The Client Experience:
How to Optimize Client Service and Deliver Value

AF757613

EDITED BY ALEX DAVIES

Commissioning editor
Alex Davies

Managing director
Sian O'Neill

The Client Experience: How to Optimize Client Service and Deliver Value
is published by

Globe Law and Business Ltd
3 Mylor Close
Horsell
Woking
Surrey GU21 4DD
United Kingdom
Tel: +44 20 3745 4770
www.globelawandbusiness.com

The Client Experience: How to Optimize Client Service and Deliver Value

ISBN 9781787428133
EPUB ISBN 9781787428140
Adobe PDF ISBN 9781787428157

© 2021 Globe Law and Business Ltd except where otherwise indicated.

The right of the contributors to be identified as authors of this work has been asserted by them in accordance with sections 77 and 78 of the Copyright, Designs and Patents Act 1988.

All rights reserved. No part of this publication may be reproduced in any material form (including photocopying, storing in any medium by electronic means or transmitting) without the written permission of the copyright owner, except in accordance with the provisions of the Copyright, Designs and Patents Act 1988 or under terms of a licence issued by the Copyright Licensing Agency Ltd, 5th Floor, Shackleton House, 4 Battle Bridge Lane, London SE1 2HX, United Kingdom (www.cla.co.uk, email: licence@cla.co.uk). Applications for the copyright owner's written permission to reproduce any part of this publication should be addressed to the publisher.

DISCLAIMER
This publication is intended as a general guide only. The information and opinions which it contains are not intended to be a comprehensive study, or to provide legal advice, and should not be treated as a substitute for legal advice concerning particular situations. Legal advice should always be sought before taking any action based on the information provided. The publisher bears no responsibility for any errors or omissions contained herein.

Contents

Executive summary

We all know that law is a people business. Clients buy from lawyers whom they like, respect, and trust, and they judge those lawyers and their firms on the quality of service that the firm provides, the results achieved, and whether they receive value for money. This applies to corporate, institutional, and private clients alike. For their business plans to be connected to reality, partners and law firm leaders must learn how they are perceived by their clients and adapt accordingly. They do this by listening to their clients. Historically this was through informal, fireside chats. In recent years, many firms have devised formal client listening programs and there has been an explosion of review sites and social media channels enabling clients to leave their unfiltered and public feedback, whether solicited or not. Forward-looking firms are adopting multi-channel approaches to taking feedback to maximize the intelligence they gather and to adapt to clients' own preferences. As ever, the most nimble and adaptable will reap the rewards.

Chapter one by Sally Dyson of Firm Sense Ltd explains the benefits of really listening to your clients and emphasizes the importance of listening both in good times and in bad, based on experience of engaging with clients throughout the COVID-19 pandemic. Sally highlights the interplay between client listening and optimizing client experience, reviews the modern listening methods available to firms, discusses the proliferation of review sites and how to respond to them, and finishes with a vision of how firms can integrate all their data to see the client picture in full technicolor.

Implementing a client feedback program is one of the most effective ways to ensure client service excellence. Feedback provides valuable insight into what is working and what is not, and enables concrete actions to be taken to create more value for clients and improve the end-to-end client experience. Challenging questions, a flexible questioning technique, and strong reflective listening are key. In chapter two, Will Taylor, senior client development manager at Wiersholm, looks at how a structured client listening program that digs a little deeper into the relationship and that extends beyond the "safe" client base can provide valuable insights into how to improve the client experience, both for an individual client relationship and more systemically as a firm.

In chapter three, Yolanda Cartusciello, partner at PP&C Consulting, demonstrates that differentiating the client experience is a critical component of a law firm's success, and client journey mapping is an effective tool in helping firms do this. While client journey mapping may be new to law firms, the technique has been used successfully by corporations across industries and around the world. Consumer product and B2C organizations such as Amazon, Apple, and Disney, as well as B2B and consulting firms such as IBM and McKinsey, have focused on the client journey as a way of improving and distinguishing the client experience. PP&C Consulting has translated and adapted this technique for the law firm environment, mapping the technique with law firm practice and industry groups, as well as in business development training programs, to help lawyers and firms better understand the experiences they deliver and how those experiences might be improved.

This process is continued in chapter four by Andrew Hedley of Hedley Consulting. As the end-to-end management of the client experience builds momentum as a source of strategic advantage, client journey mapping is becoming *de rigueur* as a key tool. Leading firms are using journey mapping techniques to bring clarity to their market positioning, says Andrew, building sustainable competitive advantage with increasingly discerning clients. Put simply, client journey mapping is a technique for charting the client's interactions with the business from first becoming aware of the firm, through initial appointment, and ongoing engagement. By better understanding the client's "touch points" with the firm – whether physical or virtual – action can be taken to ensure consistency of service experience. It is at these touch points that perceptions and reputations are created and built (or destroyed) for clients and prospects. However, the touch point experience is shaped by the firm's service strategy, structures, and processes. What is critical here is a coherent strategy, a well communicated and understood service delivery model, clear expectations in relation to "what good looks like", and an underpinning infrastructure that supports excellent service delivery and superb experience creation. Andrew sets out the strategic rationale for client journey mapping, providing pointers for law firm leaders wishing to introduce the approach as part of a wider business development strategy.

With input from an all-star team of law firm marketing and business development "masters", the next chapter from David H. Freeman, chief executive officer of the David Freeman Consulting Group, discusses what it means to become a trusted advisor and presents real-world approaches for enhancing relationships by delivering value beyond the client's expectations. Great service is not just a "nice-to-have," maintains David – there is a clear link between high levels of client service and financial rewards, with research showing that firms with consistently superior client service enjoy hourly rate premiums, higher profits per partner, and greater client retention.

Indeed, delivering a "stellar service" is essential for customer-focused, modern law firms such as FBC Manby Bowdler LLP, which has put the client journey at the center of everything it does. To ensure the principles of its client service charter are upheld, the firm uses regular customer audits to measure and respond to performance – celebrating the positives and acting on constructive feedback – while introducing a number of technology-based solutions to make its service and communications more efficient, cost effective, and accessible for clients. In chapter six, Kim Carr, lead partner of the wills, probate and lifetime planning department at FBC Manby Bowdler LLP, explains how it's done.

Client service has never been so important. After such a traumatic year, clients need to know their legal advisers have their best interests at heart. This not only means continuing to deliver excellent work, it also means providing excellent service. If you can give your clients the best possible experience every time they work with you and, wherever possible, exceed their expectations, you will reinforce your existing relationships and maximize referral levels so you have a pipeline of prospective clients that will underpin the next phase of your firm's growth. In chapter seven, Douglas McPherson, director of Size 10½ Boots Ltd, looks at the commercial benefits of optimizing client service (and conversely the potential risks to a practice if client service isn't optimized), how to highlight where improvements can be made, and how practically to implement those improvements, especially given most firms will have to manage the process around the new hybrid working environment.

Over the last few years, the concept of LegalTech has really taken hold. Up to this point it has largely been equated with workflow, delivery, and improving internal efficiencies. However, a raft of more accessible, more implementable, and more affordable technologies is poised to transform client care. These solutions have been designed to enable law firms to enhance their client experience and increase the volume of new enquires (and the rate at which these enquiries are converted into billable work). At the forefront of this online revolution are virtual assistants.

Virtual assistants can be added to any law firm's website search bar and programmed to give visitors the care, attention, and answers they want, irrespective of when they visit and what they want to find out. From the perspective of the law firm, they will capture more prospective clients and direct them – faster and more efficiently – towards conversion. In chapter eight, James Matthews of CM.com explores the different ways in which virtual assistants allow law firms to not only optimize the level of client care their website offers, but also the tangible business development and financial benefits that adding them to a website will deliver.

According to Scott Rechtschaffen, chief knowledge officer at Littler Mendelson, "a true innovation strategy envisions dramatically and comprehensively changing the way firms interact with and serve their clients". Chapter nine describes how, over the past two decades, Littler Mendelson has used its innovation strategy as a true differentiator, to improve the delivery of legal services and positively impact the law firm–client relationship – to the benefit of both.

A client-centric business model is essential for future law firm success, according to one of the sector's largest research projects undertaken by LawNet as part of the delivery and audit of its Mark of Excellence. Since 2013, LawNet's network members have taken part in regular client experience reviews, with a mix of telephone calls, web enquiries, walk-ins, and out-of-hours calls, combined with online benchmarked customer satisfaction surveying, to identify and measure strengths and weaknesses, and overall satisfaction levels. In chapter ten, Helen Hamilton-Shaw, member engagement and strategy director at LawNet, talks through the results, which are used to guide future support and developments across the network and within individual firms.

Litigation historically surges after crises and economic recession, and the surge is on even as the COVID-19 pandemic continues to plague the globe with the virus variants. Companies must prepare because pandemic litigation is already here and more is on the way. In our final chapter, Shook, Hardy & Bacon LLP partner and general liability litigation practice co-chair Paul A. Williams presents an overview of the COVID-19 pandemic-driven litigation trends, forecasts what's yet to come, and offers an approach to litigation management that can improve the client's experience and mitigate the burden and disruption traditionally associated with it. Sophisticated litigation management begins with identifying risks and limiting exposure by establishing clear legal and business objectives to guide business strategy. A company can then leverage the best features of right-fit teams and available time-saving processes and technologies to achieve efficient and effective outcomes across its litigation portfolio. With a client-focused partner, companies are empowered to anticipate and control litigation spend and strategically manage their litigation outcomes, while also achieving a better overall litigation experience in an environment compatible with the company's culture and business objectives. In short, an approach that can provide a bit of client certainty in a still uncertain world.

About the authors

Kim Carr is lead partner of the wills, probate, and lifetime planning department at FBC Manby Bowdler LLP. Ranked in both the Legal 500 and *Chambers*, FBC Manby Bowdler LLP is a 28-partner firm with over 170 staff working from six offices across the West Midlands, Shropshire, and Worcestershire in the UK. Kim first joined the firm as a trainee solicitor in 1986 and later progressed to partner and then managing partner before taking the position as lead partner for the wills, probate, and lifetime planning department in April 2020. Kim was named LawNet Managing Partner of the Year in 2012 and has been chair of the LawNet board since 2015 – the first woman to hold the role in the network's 26-year history.

For more than 20 years, **Yolanda Cartusciello** served in senior administrative leadership roles in major law firms, including Debevoise & Plimpton and Cleary Gottlieb. At both firms, she led the marketing teams, designed their business development and media strategies and took charge of their implementation. She was the chief architect of profile enhancement strategies, perception studies, branding exercises, comprehensive client interview programs, and practice and lateral partner rollouts. She co-developed marketing technology solutions and created media relations and digital strategies. She has also developed business development and communications training and coaching programs for lawyers at all levels. For the last five years of her tenure at Debevoise, Yolanda was a permanent participant in the weekly management committee meetings and worked on a number of firm committees and projects, including an evaluation of all of the partner-facing support functions of the firm. Since joining PP&C Consulting in January 2016, Yolanda has undertaken a number of strategic planning projects, working with firm management to adopt firmwide, practice- and office-specific strategies. She has also performed marketing function analyses, including a review of people, processes, and technology. Yolanda has also helped to launch several smaller firms, leading the marketing and business development rollout and providing overall administrative direction. In addition, Yolanda has long experience handling organizational and personnel issues. She has advised on the development of the legal assistant, knowledge, and practice management, and legal marketing staff roles at various firms. She hired, trained, and supervised more than 150 administrative employees for work in high-achieving cultures. Yolanda has a BA from the University of Iowa and an MFA from Brooklyn College.

Sally Dyson is the director of Firm Sense Ltd, a legal sector specialist consultancy where she provides a combination of client listening, executive coaching, and business skills training to enhance her clients' personal and business effectiveness and to enable them to create and implement client-focused success strategies. Sally's experience working both as a private practice solicitor and as an in-house lawyer inspired her to found Firm Sense to bridge the communication gap between lawyers and their clients. In addition to her legal qualifications, Sally is a trained coach and author of several books for lawyers: *Client Listening: Why it Pays and How to Do it*, *Budgeting and Negotiating Fees with Clients: A Lawyer's Guide* and *The Real Deal: Law Firm Leadership that Works*.

David H. Freeman, JD is an award-winning consultant and two-time bestselling author, and for 27 years has trained and coached thousands of lawyers and leaders from hundreds of law firms worldwide, including nearly half of the Am Law 200. He is a former practicing lawyer from New York, and for three consecutive years he was voted the #1 business development consultant and coach in nationwide *National Law Journal* surveys, which earned him the distinction of being named to the *National Law Journal* Hall of Fame. He is also a fellow in the College of Law Practice Management. David is the CEO of the David Freeman Consulting Group, founder of Law Firm CultureShift®, the creator of the Culture Xray® (an internal business development culture assessment), and the developer of breakthrough technology that automates cross-selling coaching for lawyers (Cross Serving®). David is also the author and co-author of 13 books on law firm business development, leadership, and client service, and is a frequent speaker at industry conferences and law firm retreats.

Helen Hamilton-Shaw, member engagement and strategy director with LawNet, is recognized as a driving force in legal sector client experience, having designed and developed LawNet's award-winning Mark of Excellence in client care. LawNet provides a vibrant community for progressive, independent law firms aspiring to excellence and gives its members access to collective purchasing, shared knowledge, best practice, and expertise. Members of the collaborative, mutually-owned, national network range from £2m to £25m turnover and must achieve and maintain LawNet's own ISO 9001 standard and the associated Mark of Excellence in client service.

Andrew Hedley is a prominent advisor to the legal, accounting, and property sectors. He works with firm leaders on issues of vision, strategy, growth, profit enhancement, performance improvement, merger, and change management. In addition to project work, he is also much sought after as a strategy group guide, partner retreat speaker, workshop facilitator, and moderator. Andrew is a respected contributor to specialist strategy and management publications. He is a regular keynote conference speaker, media commentator, and regularly writes within the sector media.

He is the author of *Developing Strategic Client Relationships, Client Strategy in a Changing Legal Market* and *The Law Firm Merger: A Leader's Guide to Strategy and Realisation*. He sits on the advisory board of the Managing Partners' Forum and chairs the MPF Awards for Management Excellence judging panel. Andrew has been admitted as a fellow of the Institute of Directors, the Strategic Planning Society, the Chartered Management Institute, the Chartered Institute of Marketing, Cambridge Marketing College, and the Royal Society of Art. He is a member of the Triple Nine Society and sits on the Council of The Naval Club. His firm, Hedley Consulting, is recognized as a leading boutique strategy consultancy to the professional services sector, with clients ranging from global firms to significant regional players.

James Matthews is the country manager of CM.com in the UK and Ireland and leads the team's expansion across the region, championing the benefits of cloud software for conversational commerce. Passionate about technology since the very start of his career and armed with a Bachelor's Degree in Marketing from the University of Portsmouth, James cut his teeth at Motorola before moving into sales roles at Sony and Canon. His passion for technology took him to Telephonetics VIP (now Netcall) where he was immersed in the cut and thrust of customer contact and automation for both the private and public sector.

Leading the corporate team at Truphone – one of Europe's best-funded start-ups – James was responsible for three sales teams (Corporate, SME and Channel). He enjoyed great success building Truphone's sales organization, selling Truphone's innovative technology services to some of the largest corporations and enterprises both in the UK and US. Bitten by the start-up bug, he joined Route Mobile as VP for Europe, selling SaaS and CPaaS solutions alongside customer support and operations services. As the first person in the region, James built a formidable team across Europe in sales, marketing, and tech support. Route Mobile recently IPO'd.

Joining CM.com in 2020, his wealth of experience in sales, marketing, and customer service – not to mention his invaluable start-up background – is the driving factor in the company's continued growth across the UK and Ireland, working with public and private sector organizations across a wide variety of industries.

Douglas McPherson has had a long career in marketing and business development within professional services. For the last ten years he has been a director of Size 10½ Boots Ltd, a specialist BD agency that works solely with law firms, accountants, intellectual property firms, and barristers' chambers, helping them find smarter, easier, and more effective ways to grow their practice.

As Littler's chief knowledge officer, **Scott Rechtschaffen** leads the firm's effort to provide innovative client services by integrating new technologies and work processes and enabling attorneys and clients to access the collective knowledge and experience of the firm's 1,500+ attorneys. Scott heads the firm's KM department, a team of 65+ professionals including dedicated, full-time knowledge management attorneys along with legal research specialists and writers, content administrators, and a training/video production team. Scott is the co-founder of ComplianceHR, an innovative joint venture launched in 2015 by Littler and Neota Logic, a legal software company. ComplianceHR leverages Littler's experience and knowledge of employment law with the power of Neota Logic's expert systems to provide a transformative suite of online compliance solutions. Scott is also an adjunct professor of law at Cornell Tech in New York City where he teaches a class on delivering legal services through technology.

Scott has written extensively and has published articles in national publications on human resources management, knowledge management, and legal technology. He regularly speaks at knowledge management seminars and legal technology conferences organized by the American Bar Association's Law Practice Management Section, Association of Corporate Counsel, American Lawyer Media, Legal Marketing Association, International Legal Technology Association, Ark Publishing, and other professional organizations. For his achievements in knowledge management, Scott has been awarded the Distinguished Peer Award as KM Champion of the Year by the International Legal Technology Association. In 2014, he was named to the Fastcase 50 and the *Financial Times* named Scott among the ten most innovative lawyers in North America. That year, he also received an Innovator Award from *The Recorder* legal newspaper and the following year *The Recorder* awarded him for being a Serial Innovator. Scott was inducted as a fellow in the College of Law Practice Management, a peer-nominated honor bestowed on law practice management specialists, and currently serves on the College's board of trustees.

Will Taylor is a senior client development manager at Wiersholm, one of Norway's leading law firms based in Oslo, and has a decade of experience working in business development and client development roles, predominantly in the legal sector. He has broad international experience, having worked at market-leading law firms in London and Auckland, as well as within legal roles in Australia, India, and China. His experience includes client feedback, end-to-end pitch management, client experience, pricing, business planning, thought leadership, and training. He has written a number of articles and chapters on client experience topics. He has a degree and Masters in law.

Paul A. Williams is a partner at Shook, Hardy & Bacon LLP and co-chair of Shook's general liability litigation practice group, based in Kansas City. He focuses his trial practice on complex litigation and trial practice management and partners with clients to create relationships that align client and firm interests to achieve better legal outcomes at exceptional value. Paul believes win-win partnerships with clients are built on collaboration, innovation, strategic action, and trust – all of which ultimately bring better results and the metrics to prove them. He has received national recognition for his innovative use of alternative billing arrangements and the Coefficient® litigation management approach to curtail legal spend and effectively manage otherwise unpredictable litigation. Paul has been named as an Acritas Star, a Client Service All-Star by BTI Consulting, and as a Litigation Trailblazer by *National Law Journal* for his client-first focused relationships and his leadership in alternative fee arrangements.

Chapter 1: Client feedback has gone stereophonic: are you still listening in mono?

By Sally Dyson, director, Firm Sense Ltd

Introduction

The case for client listening is compelling. The myriad potential benefits, if well executed include:

- Spotting opportunities to solve client problems, developing new service lines and winning additional business;
- Improving client relationships;
- Benchmarking performance against competitors;
- Appraising performance of individuals, setting goals and constructing evidence-based business plans; and
- Contributing towards the achievement of quality certifications such as ISO accreditations.[1]

One of the reasons that firms need to listen to their clients is to verify that the claims they make about themselves are true. A managing partner may have risen to the top of the firm owing to a mix of technical expertise, reliable execution, lucrative client relationships, and a wide network of supporters. But what about the other partners and employees of the firm? They won't all be providing the same outstanding performance. A firm leader must not assume that the experience of working with the firm is uniformly excellent or even consistent across practice groups, offices, and jurisdictions. Without understanding what it is like to be a client, the firm cannot set itself robust, realistic targets for development or deliver on its brand promises.

Of course, client listening should not just be a backwards look at prior performance, useful though that is. To really make a difference, an open dialogue between clients and law firms, sometimes mediated by third party interviewers, explores clients' current and likely future needs and priorities to adapt approaches and co-create strategies and solutions.

Whilst firms continue to agonize about whether to approach their clients for feedback and, if so, how and when to do it, firms will increasingly find themselves the recipients of both solicited and unsolicited feedback on comparison websites and digital review platforms. Meanwhile, regulators are considering how such platforms can be harnessed to meet their policy objectives of enhancing transparency and consumer protection and the extent to which there should be an element of compulsion for firms to play ball. The question is no longer whether to obtain feedback but which channels to emphasize and how to integrate feedback from multiple sources to drive action that delivers positive change.

This chapter will describe the different ways in which firms are now obtaining feedback; explain how client listening has been super-charged during the COVID-19 pandemic; outline how this dovetails with regulatory initiatives in England and Wales, and offer some solutions for firms that are trying to integrate and navigate a deluge of disparate data to inform strategy and set service standards.

How firms listen

Successful professionals have always found ways to listen to their clients and to use that feedback to shape the services that they provide. Historically, active solicitation of feedback mostly took the form of private conversations, often over a meal and a drink, and the timing and approach would have been at individual partner discretion with the responses known only to the partner, who was free to use or ignore the snippets gleaned, leaving colleagues none the wiser.

Today, as a more managerial approach is taken to running law firms and with the introduction of cadres of professional business development and marketing managers and the appointment of executive leaders such as managing partners or even chief executives, finance and operating officers, firms have introduced more systemized (if not yet systematic) methods.

There are many different sources of feedback available to law firms. Research by MyCustomerLens (featured later in this chapter) in collaboration with Inpractice, a business development consultancy, asked 29 law firms to identify the most common methods they used to obtain feedback. The results are shown in Figure 1. Some of these methods require firms to invite feedback proactively, with varying degrees of formality and planning whereas, in other cases, feedback may be proffered at the client's initiative. This chapter will focus on client interviews, surveys, market research, online reviews, and social media.

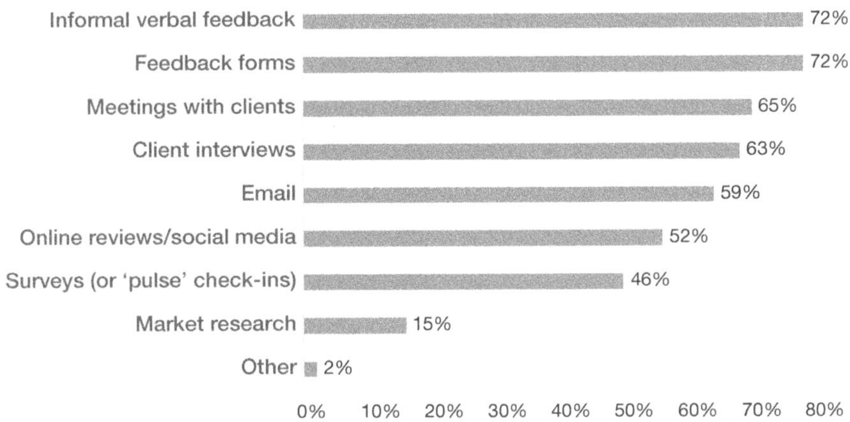

Figure 1: Sources of feedback used by firms, Voice of the Client Benchmarking Study, June 2021 by MyCustomerLens and Inpractice, reproduced with permission.

Client interviews and surveys are two of the most important ways in which firms run feedback campaigns and the advantages and disadvantages of each are briefly examined below.

Depth interviews

Interviews are the method of choice for ascertaining the views of high status and hard to reach individuals. This might include general counsel and other senior personnel of commercial or public sector clients. Interviews are flexible and tailored to the interests of the interviewee, allowing for wide-ranging discussion, delivering candid insights once rapport has been built with the interviewee, providing reassurance that they have been understood, and sending a powerful signal that they are valued. Interviews can capture the nuance of complex issues and can probe "why" clients feel or act a particular way, not just "what" they do. However, interviews are time consuming to conduct and even more so to write-up, analyze, and compare with other interviews and so they tend to be reserved for key clients or for specific projects. Most firms will only interview a client after obtaining permission from the client relationship partner and these partners often feel sensitive about the timing of any approaches to their clients, finding reasons to delay. There can also be a disconnect between the person who takes the feedback and the people who are tasked with responding to it so that valuable insights may remain buried in a file.

Surveys

The plethora of digital tools, many offering a free-of-charge basic service, have made it easier than ever for firms to canvas feedback from their clients, capture and organize the responses and share the outputs, all at the touch of a few buttons. Surveys are excellent for obtaining a snapshot of information from a large number of people at speed. Surveys lend themselves better to statistical and comparative analysis within firms over time and against other firms but they lack the rich detail and personalization of interviews. Additionally, not everyone can design an excellent survey – "rubbish in, rubbish out" as the saying goes. Completing a survey generally feels like a chore or a favor performed for the firm unless the firm can clearly express the purpose of the survey and how it will ultimately benefit the client. Poorly designed questions that confuse will undermine the reliability of any findings and over-use or tedious questions that bore the user result in low completion rates.

For a number of years, debate has centered on whether to interview or to survey clients and how to gain partner buy-in and participation. The ideal answer is that firms should use both, depending on the nature of their objectives, the seniority of the person being approached, and by segmenting their audience so that individuals are not bombarded with overlapping requests. In fact, firms do not simply face a binary choice between interviews and surveys. Firms are likely to be participating in a number of other feedback-gathering mechanisms, willingly or not, and it is now becoming a matter of how to engage with and optimize the benefits of these channels.

Directories

When I started out as an in-house lawyer, the world was transitioning from clunky dial-up internet and most forms of legal research still involved turning pages of weighty tomes in law libraries. When looking for a new external counsel in an obscure specialty or unfamiliar country the doorstop-sized legal directories, such as *The Legal 500* and *Chambers and Partners* provided information that was hard to obtain elsewhere. Despite the profusion of online data sources now available, the directory publishers have succeeded in maintaining their status, at least in the sense that few commercial law firms dare not to perform the annual routine of directory submissions. It is a rigmarole that law firm marketeers dread as they complete the time-consuming forms and marshal referees. I asked Vikki Bentwood, veteran of many rounds of directory submissions and founder of legal marketing consultancy, The Legal Linchpin, whether the directories were more than marketing puff for law firms. In her view, the directories are "proud of their research and time spent in the market" but the perception of the directories may be muddied by the co-existence of their editorial and sales arms. Whilst the *Legal 500*, for example, emphasizes that firms "can't buy into editorial" they can purchase and draft their own profile pages and those that do so are more prominently featured. For some firms, the directories are only about building their brands and advertising their credentials but the research process involves interviewing and surveying clients and taking soundings from other market participants such as barristers and these research reports can provide firms, that are willing to pay for them, with valuable client insights. Vikki recounts that firms that do purchase the research reports have sometimes been surprised to receive criticism as well as praise from their hand-selected referees. This mirrors my own experience of carrying out client listening interviews on behalf of firms where praise is leavened with constructive criticism and points towards areas for development. Any kind of negative comment can be difficult to accept, initially, but firms tell me that this is where the real value lies. Unlike client listening commissioned by a firm, where consent can be obtained to report client comments on an attributed basis, a difficulty with the directory feedback is that it is anonymized. There are sound reasons for the directories taking this approach but it does deprive firms of context, which can help make critiques land with greater legitimacy, and also removes any direct right of reply or ability for lawyers to work collaboratively with individual clients to create remedies for deficiencies. Whether due to budget constraints or a failure to recognize what they are missing, undoubtedly some firms are leaving this valuable intelligence on the table.

COVID-19 induced acceleration

A huge 86 percent of respondents to a 2021 survey said that client listening would become more important to their firm.[2] In a period of rapid change and uncertainty, firms need to keep up to date with their clients' evolving priorities and needs. As the pandemic threw the world into turmoil in early 2020, clients raced to review their commercial contracts and to get to grips with the different jurisdictional approaches to *force majeure* clauses and employment rights. Landlords and tenants negotiated rent holidays and banks were called upon to provide liquidity and restructure debt. Disputes naturally emerged. However, despite the pandemic continuing to rage over a long duration and leaving no one untouched, the impacts were not felt universally in the same way. After an initial period of firefighting, for some clients the situation settled down whereas others, for example in the travel and hospitality sectors, faced continually changing regulations, taking them repeatedly to cliff edges and requiring them to constantly make and unmake plans to revive their businesses. No wonder that a one-size fits all approach would have been inappropriate and firms recognized that the only way to provide an appropriately tailored response was to talk to their clients. As Sadie Baron, chief marketing officer at Reed Smith said to me:[3]

> *"Every conversation we've had with a client we've used as an excuse to be client listening, to not only go with the ideas that we've got, and there have been plenty, but to also capture high-level conversations with clients, how they're doing, how the business is doing, any pinch points they're having at the moment, and feeding that back in to our client partners that these are the pain points that other clients are seeing, that we could be helping with."*

I certainly found clients of law firms very receptive to engaging in client listening throughout the pandemic and heard for myself how the focus of their concerns and the type of support they needed from their law firms varied over the course of 2020 and 2021. At the start of the crisis, many were battening down the hatches, looking inwards at a damage limitation exercise, but as time passed optimism revived and businesses that had weathered the storm were raising finance and searching for investment opportunities and therefore calling for very different kinds of legal support. Naturally, my own client listening endeavors had to move online. Like everybody else, Zoom, Microsoft Teams, and Google Meets became my friends and enablers. A very noticeable upside was that despite many people working longer hours, under intense pressure, with a blurring of home and work boundaries, I experienced a huge willingness from lawyers and their clients to accept invitations to participate in video calls. The barriers to conducting client listening interviews very much diminished as participants recognized the need for up-to-date sharing of information and a chance to express their feelings but also found video calls to be less intrusive and time consuming than meetings whilst providing more opportunities for social bonding and rapport to develop than during phone calls.

Digital platforms

The widespread adoption of video calling technology was just one of the most remarked-upon and widely experienced innovations of the pandemic that thrust digitization into warp speed. In countless conversations, both law firm leaders and their clients told me that changes that they had been planning but been unsure how to get approved or implemented had taken place in a matter of weeks at the start of the pandemic as the crisis forced the pace. With people compelled to physically isolate from each other, the digital platforms took on a new significance that is likely here to stay. Clients are able to express themselves publicly as never before but not all firms are properly exploiting these seams of data. The next paragraphs examine how social media and review websites are democratizing the client listening and feedback process.

Social media

Many lawyers are wary of bringing social media into their professional lives, but if they tolerate one platform, it is likely to be the business networking site, LinkedIn. Individuals will have personal profiles on the site and, in all probability, their firms will also have company pages. The extent to which they leverage this resource varies. As with all digital platforms, providers are constantly innovating, and that means that the array of tools and features is regularly updated. What was once in vogue can rapidly become old hat but the platform provides opportunities for clients and colleagues to offer various kinds of endorsements, recommendations, and public thanks. Social media has many, well publicized, flaws but it is also an incredibly powerful tool for customer engagement. One of the greatest benefits of social media is that it is not just a shop window through which to display wares or a podium from which to broadcast, although it can be both but, at its essence, it is designed to share information, to foster conversation, and to connect people. Lawyers with business, charity, and public sector clients can learn a huge amount about the institutions they serve and the individuals who instruct them by following their LinkedIn posts. They will learn if a deal has just closed, a new office has opened, a member of staff has left or joined, or a new product has been launched. From time to time they'll learn about happy or tragic personal developments. They might hear about frustrations suffered and solutions found and all of this will help them to provide a better service and to display empathy. They shouldn't just squirrel away the information but share the intelligence with their colleagues and respond via the site or through their regular communication channels to demonstrate their awareness and to provide support.

Law firms have been slower to harness the power of Facebook, perhaps viewing it as genuinely "social" media and too trivial for the serious business of the law. Consumer businesses, of course, know better and the largest have attracted millions of followers to their pages. Facebook has a review function, which businesses can choose whether to display, but this appears slow to have gained traction within the legal community when compared with some of the review sites described below. Important as these review sites are, they are not the only way that the internet has opened up a wealth of opportunities for business owners and law firms to understand their clients. Some firms have started client special interest groups. An example is the Irwin Mitchell parent carer forum. It is a private members group (you have to apply to join) designed to be a safe space in which members of the public, who may or may not be clients of the firm but have common interests or attributes (in this case they are parent carers), can connect online to discuss the issues that matter to them. The group is run by the firm and they say that "our solicitors and client liaison specialists are here to support you". Clients and potential clients may be drawn to the helpfulness of the firm and the sense of community and loyalty that it engenders, making the firm a natural choice for those people to turn to when they need advice. Meanwhile, the firm has multiple interactions with its target audience and learns dynamically about what keeps them awake at night and can scope its service design around this knowledge.

Firms don't have to host their own discussion groups. There are plenty of special interest groups that they can join as demonstrated in the case study on Artistic Brief, a legal consultancy serving the creative sector.

CASE STUDY

CASE STUDY: Artistic Brief Limited

About the firm: Artistic Brief is a new breed of legal and creative consultancy led by Janine Collins, an SRA-regulated independent solicitor, authorized to provide selected legal services through a limited company.[4] In the legal sphere, Artistic Brief provides corporate and commercial advice to small businesses and individuals in the creative industries.

Facebook listening: Immersing herself in the world of creative industries, Janine joined several Facebook business groups in which members ask each other questions and seek advice and support. Taking part in these online conversations gave Janine a window into the business issues and legal preoccupations of a large number of potential clients. This is an active, even interactive, form of client listening where Janine learns about the unmet needs of her target audience and provides value in advance of any paid engagement. As a result, Janine has often been asked by the group administrators to present talks to their groups on the legal topics that are regularly raised by members, such as understanding essential clauses for terms of business or how to protect intellectual property. These talks are generally live streamed and then replayed many times by popular demand. Each interaction with a group member, response to a query, or talk delivered tends to prompt other group members to approach Janine for further advice. They are not shy about letting her know when her advice has been helpful. She estimates that around 20 percent of her clients have found her via these Facebook interactions.

Comparison and review sites

The legal market is not working in the interests of consumers. This was the conclusion of a market study performed by the Competition and Markets Authority (CMA) in 2016,[5] which they reconfirmed in 2020,[6] and charged the Legal Services Board (LSB) with coordinating progress. In turn, the LSB's 2020 research found that, every year, 3.6 million people in England and Wales have an unmet need involving a legal dispute. Their research participants suggested that star ratings would be the most helpful, "at a glance" way that they could judge the quality of legal services and that they would see the experience of other customers as the most important indicator of a high-quality provider. Following from this, in September 2021 the LSB launched a consultation[7] on a draft statutory statement of policy on empowering consumers in which it states that:

> *"We consider that consumers need information about the price, quality, and service of legal providers, as well as information on regulation and redress, so that they are best equipped to shop around and make effective choices…"*

With the COVID-19 pandemic forcing far more people to work, research, and shop online, enormous numbers of people have come to rely on comparison sites such as Compare the Market or Money Supermarket before making a substantial purchase, so it is obvious that they will look for similar comparative information when selecting a solicitor.

In response, in 2021, the SRA, acting with the Council for Licensed Conveyancers and the professional body for chartered legal executives "CILEx", launched a pilot scheme with various law firms and comparison website providers to investigate how reliable comparative information can best be made available to the public.[8] Whilst the motivation of the regulators is to improve transparency in the legal market, the comparison and review sites provide an incredible opportunity for law firms to receive constantly updated intelligence and feedback from their clients. This work has led the SRA to identify and respond to a series of common concerns raised by law firms.

Regulatory obligations

SRA Regulation 5.1 requires information to be provided to clients if firms have paid referral fees to procure their business. The SRA has provided reassurance that the business models of most comparison sites do not trigger Regulation 5.1, for example if the firm pays a subscription regardless of the number of leads provided or if payments are made per introduction, regardless of whether the client ultimately instructs the firm. Please be aware that a separate regime applies to personal injury work, which is not included in the SRA pilot. In all cases, firms should check the SRA website for more information.

Negative reviews

Firms understandably worry about negative reviews and these are bound to crop up from time to time. Taking advantage of the fact that comparison sites, like social media sites, allow for two-way interaction, the SRA advice is emphatic that firms should respond to negative reviews (taking care neither to divulge confidential information, nor to pressurize clients to retract their reviews). Their research has found that 80 percent of consumers believe businesses that respond to reviews (both positive and negative) care more about them and 45 percent of consumers are more likely to visit businesses that respond to reviews. Businesses that proactively handle complaints are on average two to three percent more profitable.[9] Generally, the most effective approach is to acknowledge that a reviewer is dissatisfied and invite them to discuss the issue privately with the firm in order to achieve resolution. It is well known that prospective clients take note of how firms respond to negative reviews and sometimes firms even win business from clients who have been impressed by this display of good customer service.

Fake reviews

Fake, possibly malicious, reviews are another concern and may be more of an issue on Google Reviews than some other sites. All of the sites involved in the SRA pilot are committed to only allowing reviews from genuine clients (or prospective clients that have interacted with the firm to an extent) and the SRA has produced a code of conduct that they have all agreed to abide by. Suspected fake reviews can be flagged to the providers who will investigate and remove them if found not to be genuine.

VHS or Betamax

With so many comparison and review sites springing up, law firms may not know which ones to ally themselves to. There are of course differences between the sites. They offer a variety of free of charge and paid for services and integrations. Some cover a multitude of industries such as Trust Pilot. These may have greater name recognition amongst the public and might be a consumer's natural first port of call. Others are legal sector specific, for example, ReviewSolicitors which, by September 2021, had signed-up 1,800 law firms and states that its reviews are seen by 4.5 million clients per year.[10] Trust Pilot and ReviewSolicitors are amongst a number of providers participating in the SRA pilot and have signed-up to the SRA's voluntary code of conduct.

Review sites linked to internet search engines, notably the ubiquitous Google Reviews, are an important source of law firm reviews. Given that Google is the most commonly used search engine and that many buyers will begin their quest to find legal advice with a Google search, it is a force to be reckoned with. Not only that but Google's algorithm treats online reviews as an important ranking factor in search optimization so a higher volume of four- and five-star reviews will get your firm noticed. In acknowledgement of this, some comparison sites such as ReviewSolicitors offer hybrid solutions by incorporating Google Reviews in their feeds. Most sites will alert firms when a new review has been posted so that tracking multiple sites is made simpler than it would otherwise be. In reality, firms may have less of a choice than they imagine. Very often, clients, counterparties, employees, and visitors can leave reviews whether invited by the firm to do so or not, as brought to life in the case study below on Blacks Solicitors and our section on the relevance of review sites to law firms that primarily service the business market.

CASE STUDY

CASE STUDY: Blacks Solicitors LLP

About the firm: Blacks is a UK firm, based in Yorkshire, with 25 partners and 180 staff and serving both commercial and private clients. It offers the spectrum of corporate, commercial, property, disputes, employment, and insolvency work as well as consumer areas such as family, wills, and conveyancing. Its specialist sector expertise includes healthcare, education, leisure, and hospitality (including holiday and home parks and hotels) and sport. The firm prides itself on its four-hour call-back promise.

Review site ratings: At the time of writing,[11] Blacks had garnered an enviable number of favorable reviews across a variety of digital comparison and review platforms. One reason for the volume of reviews is that Blacks has a large residential conveyancing practice. Clients in this field seem more likely to post reviews than clients of other practice areas. Buying or selling a home is a major milestone for most people; they are usually delighted to reach completion, the process is quite involved, allowing time for a relationship to develop between lawyers and clients, yet the subject matter is not overly sensitive. The other reason is that the firm remembers to ask its clients to consider leaving a review.

Site	Number of reviews	Rating
Trust Pilot	837	★★★★½
ReviewSolicitors	307	★★★★½
Google Reviews	348	★★★★

Engagement with review sites: Chris Allen, managing partner, explained that he started to take an interest in social media around 12 years ago. He first embraced Twitter as a worldwide, free of charge, instant-access marketing platform. Taking a leaf out of the book of his hospitality and leisure clients, he started to invite clients to leave Google Reviews and encouraged his colleagues to ask the same of their clients. The firm never tells its clients what to write and does not get any option to pre-approve text. Chris is not afraid of the occasional negative review. He knows that these are vastly outweighed by positives. The firm came later to Trust Pilot and ReviewSolicitors. Chris became aware that the firm had attracted a few poor ratings on the Trust Pilot site. Some of these may have been from transaction counterparties rather than clients of the firm. He countered this simply by asking clients to consider posting either a Google Review or a review on Trust Pilot. Clients naturally gravitated to one or the other and, over time, the firm built up a large number of positive reviews and currently the firm is well represented on all three of the review sites discussed in this chapter. Meanwhile, Chris has continued to experiment with Twitter, Instagram, LinkedIn and, most recently, podcasting.

Where B2C leads, B2B follows

It is unsurprising that law firms catering for consumer and small- to medium-sized businesses are currently far more engaged with review and comparison sites than blue chip corporate firms. This does not mean that these august institutions are entirely invisible on the digital platforms. Many have some kind of a presence, whether they are aware of it and choose to curate it or not. The quality of the Google Reviews, in particular, for these kinds of firms is currently woeful, and often comical, exemplified by choice nuggets such as this, about my alma mater, City stalwart Slaughter and May: "Very nice place. Lots of lawyers inside." Or this about Magic Circle firm, Linklaters: "The law's an ass. And they kick it. For a price."

Whilst no one would seriously argue that these reviews would have any bearing on an institutional buyer's law firm selection, it is my contention that where the consumer firms lead, the commercial firms will follow. Companies large and small are staffed and led by people and these people increasingly shop online, check TripAdvisor before they travel, and leave reviews on Amazon. They benefit from the transparency brought by these sites and once their peers start to leave meaningful reviews in sufficient numbers, the momentum will build.

Bringing it all together

Sharing, comparing, and acting on this feedback is labor intensive and can be quite a hit and miss affair in firms where information is stored in a variety of different formats and "owned" by different individuals and departments. Figure 2 is illustrative of the wide variety of overlapping feedback repositories commonly in use in law firms with much information simply carried around in the relationship holder's head, or stored in narrowly shared documents or emails, leaving the firm vulnerable to individuals becoming incapacitated, leaving the firm, forgetting to pass, or willfully restricting access to vital information.

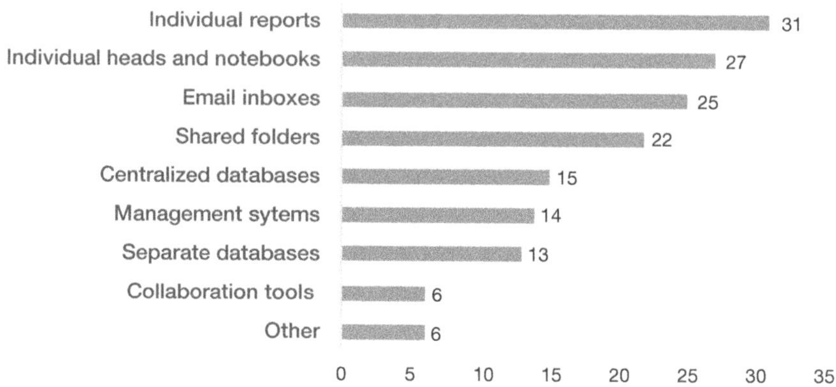

Figure 2: Stores of feedback used by firms, adapted from Voice of the Client Benchmarking Study, June 2021 by MyCustomerLens and Inpractice, reproduced with permission.

Collaboration tools

For some years, law firms have been investing in collaboration tools such as Microsoft SharePoint and client relationship management systems such as InterAction from LexisNexis. Most of these tools have the capacity to act as a central repository of information and have the ability to display client dashboards that incorporate matter and billing history, details of recent meetings, copies of interviews or survey results, and RSS news feeds. Some of these fields will populate automatically by drawing on the firm's other systems, particularly finance, and others will necessitate manual input. The success or failure of these tools rarely comes down to their technical specification and is far more likely to depend on human behavior and the ability of firm leaders to persuade their colleagues of the benefits of using the systems and regularly updating the data that they hold. The less a system relies on human effort, the better.

Automated analysis

Storing customer insights in one place is already a challenge but as the volume of data explodes, particularly narrative interview reports and unstructured reviews mined from the web, making sense of it all becomes increasingly unmanageable and requires technological solutions.

> *"Imagine if all your client listening data was in one place. Imagine if text data could be analyzed in a fast, consistent, scalable way. Imagine if your comments could be benchmarked over time and across clients."*

This is the picture painted by MyCustomerLens[12] of the benefits of using its new product to amalgamate all the feedback received by a firm from interview transcripts to survey responses to social media messages. It promises an automated analysis by algorithm to produce up-to-date online dashboards that reveal what clients are saying about a firm, how they feel, and why it drives their behavior.

Lisa Thomson, CEO at Purpose, an outsourced HR consultancy, reveals why her firm is choosing to use MyCustomerLens:

> *"As we grew our client base I was at a stage where it was no longer possible to stay connected and in touch personally on a regular basis with every client account. The system also makes it really simple and easy for our clients. Having implemented the tool, we feel like we are really listening now and the feedback is enabling us to make the right decisions across different areas of the business."*

If firms are serious about listening to clients and acting on that feedback, this kind of solution may be what they need to cut through the noise.

Conclusion

The call for client listening is loud and clear. Clients will comment on the service received from law firms, whether invited to or not, and regulators are pushing for reviews, as a source of consumer comfort, to be publicly available. Some feedback will fall on deaf ears but those firms that embrace feedback, encourage clients to leave reviews, organize their own listening exercises, and devote resource to marshalling, understanding, interpreting, and responding to their clients' voices will stay in tune with changing market expectations and customer demand.

References

1. ISO refers to the International Organization for Standardization. The ISO 9001 certification for quality management has been obtained by over one million organizations (including some law firms). A key requirement is a strong customer focus and awardees are expected to measure and monitor customer satisfaction.
2. 'The Future of Client Listening', MyCustomerLens in conjunction with Anna Lake Consulting and Client Talk, January 2021. Available at https://mycustomerlens.com.
3. First quoted in S. Dyson, "Timeless principles, updated delivery", in A. Davies (ed.), *Business Development for a New Legal Ecosystem* (Ark Publishing, 2020).
4. S10.2(a) Solicitors Regulation Authority Standards and Regulations, effective since 25 November 2019, permits SRA-regulated independent solicitors to provide

non-reserved legal services through a limited company. Reserved services are defined in the Legal Services Act 2007 and comprise a list of legal activities including conduct of litigation and probate activities that can only be provided by authorized persons.

5. CMA (2016), www.gov.uk/cma-cases/legal-servives-market-study
6. CMA (2020), www.gov.uk/government/news/cma-publishes-review-of-progress-in-legal-services-sector
7. LSB (2021), https://legalservicesboard.org.uk/wp-content/uploads/2021/09/empowering-consumers-consultation-paper-statement-of-policy.pdf
8. www.sra.org.uk/sra/news/events/on-demand-events/online-customer-reviews/
9. SRA, "Engaging with online reviews", 11 February 2021, www.sra.org.uk
10. www.reviewsolicitors.co.uk/news/2021/02/22/sra-pilot-first-look-at-the-reviewsolicitors-video
11. From information supplied to the author by MyCustomerLens.
12. Data checked 30.09.21.

Chapter 2:
Client feedback – asking the hard questions to get the best results

By Will Taylor, senior client development manager, Wiersholm

Introduction

Implementing a client feedback program is one of the most effective ways to ensure client service excellence. Feedback provides valuable insight into what is working and what is not and enables concrete actions to create more value for clients and improve the end-to-end client experience. Challenging questions, a flexible questioning technique, and strong reflective listening are key. This chapter looks at how a structured client listening program that digs a little deeper into the relationship and that extends beyond the "safe" client base can provide valuable insights into how to improve the client experience, both for an individual client relationship and more systemically as a firm.

Why have a client feedback program?

When Sophocles said, "No one loves the messenger who brings bad news" he could have been referring to the historic lack of enthusiasm towards structured client feedback programs in law firms. However, overwhelming evidence points towards the huge value gained by seeking input from clients on a systematic and ongoing basis. Whilst a lawyer or a firm may proceed on the basis that no news from a client is good news, this can sometimes overlook a more unhappy reality.

Clients do not always change law firms definitively. Instead, their discontentment can mean the next new matter ends up awarded to a different law firm, which can signal the beginning of a slippery slope out of favor, which can sometimes take years to reverse. Sometimes dissatisfied clients may simply leave the firm without providing a reason. It could be that the incumbent law firm is engaged in a long-term matter and will go on working on the matter, believing that the client is happy and has no reason to look elsewhere for an advisor, when in reality this is not correct. In order to prevent such a scenario from occurring, law firms that have not done so already should consider establishing a structured client feedback program.

Some of the benefits of such a program are summarized below.

Client retention

Client feedback can play an important role in boosting client retention, which is hugely valuable when you consider that some estimates put the cost of developing business with new clients at somewhere between five and 20 times the cost of maintaining an existing client. In an industry that puts such a strong focus on client service and where quality is often assumed and service levels are the differentiator, it provides a compelling reason for law firms to check that their clients are getting the service they require.

Revenue growth

Loyal clients will likely use law firms on more than one matter, trust them with different types of matters, and choose that firm for higher-value matters because they perceive that firm to be their preferred counsel. Loyal clients are often less price-sensitive and will often not expect automatic discounts.

Better relationships

Targeted client feedback programs create superior relationships with the most profitable clients. Asking for feedback sends a clear message that a law firm is committed to client focus and adding value to its client relationships. The client feedback session is dedicated solely to the interests of the client and demonstrates a firm's commitment to making the relationship better and not just focused on its own interest in increasing revenues.

Hidden opportunities

Why guess what a client might need assistance with when you can ask directly? If you ask the right questions and listen in the right way, the answers to these questions often develop into a discussion of areas in which the company might need legal or other services.

Demonstrating loyalty

Structured client feedback programs communicate to clients that the law firm is genuinely interested in their opinion.

Strategy

Asking clients about your performance and how you compare with your competitors can, for instance, inform decisions related to lateral hires, promoting an associate (or having a conversation about performance), or market focus. Many strategic management decisions can take direct inspiration from what a law firm's clients are telling it.

Succession planning and institutionalizing clients

Law firms must always guard against a relationship with a firm being too narrowly rooted within a firm. Partners will retire at some point, and some move on. These are often the people who have the longest and best relationship with the client. Sometimes clients who are very happy with the relationship may still express concern that more junior partners or associates are not being introduced to the relationship. Client feedback can play an important role in succession planning and help institutionalize important, long-term client relationships.

Clients want to give feedback

Many clients expect exceptional client service from their law firms and will have views on how the relationship can be improved, if only through minor adjustments. Asking clients for feedback capitalizes on other opportunities to engage and improve the relationship.

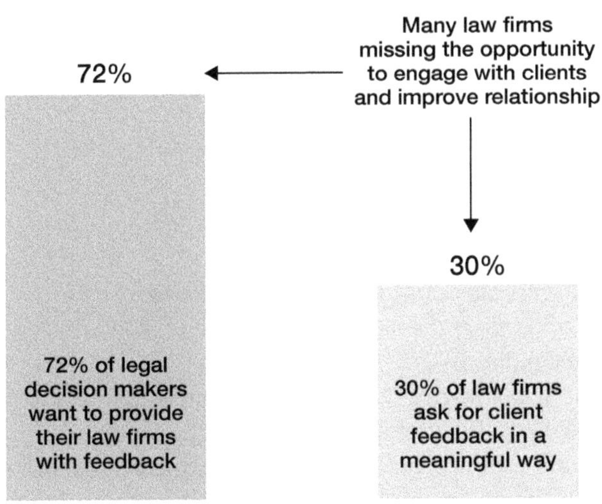

Figure 1: Law firm feedback. Source: Adapted from BTI's Annual Survey of General Counsel and Legal Decision Makers.[1]

Have a structured set of questions

The survey design process is crucial to the success of any client feedback program and worth substantial consideration. Questions should be concise and reflect both a law firm's internal strategy, values, and objectives, but also be open, show appropriate curiosity, and resonate well with clients. Priority should be placed on questions that generate actionable insights rather than large volumes of data, where the client could consider the latter a poor use of their limited time.

The survey should include direct questions related to service delivery attributes that are core to client satisfaction, such as perceived quality of work, client knowledge, and communication effectiveness. Another popular metric is likelihood to recommend, which is strongly influenced by the strength of the client relationship. This can act as a summary of overall satisfaction.

When formulating the questions, how you intend on using the feedback should be foremost in the process. It is likely the objectives will vary for different groups or clients, and the balance and versatility of the questions should reflect that. Feedback should also be realistically actionable, so the questions asked must be capable of delivering insights a firm will actually use to move toward its goals.

Regardless of the time invested and the hurdles required to agree on a set of questions, they should not be considered set in stone and inflexible. A firm's objectives or strategic direction will change over time, and the questions should be considered adaptable and evolve over time to fit a law firm's objectives.

CASE STUDY

Case Study

A hypothetical scenario could go something like this:

Interviewer: In terms of the market you operate in, how strong would you say our understanding is?

Client: Your legal advice is always extremely good and we love working with you. [Relationship Partner X] always makes sure we are well looked after. However, I would not say fintech law is a strength at your firm and you are not known in the market for this area, unlike some of your competitors. As a result, I think you sometimes misunderstand our business, and we need to explain things, but this isn't a big problem.

In fact, the firm has one of the market's leading fintech law specialists. As a result of this feedback, the firm was able to:

- Follow up with the client to identify perceived weaknesses in the fintech sector, and have the firm's fintech expert give an internal seminar to address this knowledge gap;
- Introduce the fintech specialist to the client and bring them in to matters that require strong sector knowledge, where previously a competitor performed this role, the only area they advised the client; and
- Develop a structured campaign to market the firm's expertise in fintech in order to improve its market standing in the sector.

As a result of this feedback, the law firm is able to further cement its status as the client's preferred advisor and is perceived as being able to add more value beyond the high-quality legal services the client was already satisfied with. The firm has also introduced a new revenue stream and identified a need to better communicate its expertise in fintech to the market.

Note that, on the surface, the client was very happy with its relationship with the law firm and may not have even considered that steps could be taken to improve it. It accepted the perceived weakness in the firm's capabilities as a minor inconvenience that could be overcome at little effort. It received high quality legal advice and felt prioritised. However, through asking a more targeted and challenging question, the feedback revealed that, whilst the relationship was strong, there was more that could be done to strengthen it, and at the same time weaken a competitor's position.

Ask the hard questions

To gain the most value from the client feedback, you will need to ensure that the questions are sufficiently challenging in order to deliver meaningful insights. You are unlikely to improve the client experience if you do not ask the hard questions. It can often happen that a client will offer positive feedback in response to a generic, closed question, and on that basis it is assumed that there is nothing that can or should be done differently. If you ask a "safe" question, you will often get a "safe" response.

Feedback needs to offer insights and open doors for a firm to, for example, pursue a new opportunity, make a necessary internal adjustment, or understand more about its closest competitors. Asking these questions shows enthusiasm, curiosity, and a desire to help, and is likely to impress a client far more than simpler questions.

By asking more inquisitive questions, you can start to truly look under the bonnet and uncover hidden issues. Indeed, they might not even be considered by the client to be an issue, and it may not affect day-to-day relations in any meaningful way. However, any area throughout the client journey where you can remove obstacles, even minor, can result in an improved and more enduring client relationship. The benefits can extend well beyond this, including potential new areas of revenue.

The way a question is formulated will often determine the nature of the response you get back. The most obvious example of this is using open-ended as opposed to closed questions. Using open-ended questions helps you understand things from the client's perspective as you get descriptive feedback. For example, "What do you think of the quality of our advice?" invites the interviewee to speak freely. Sometimes the interviewee will try to turn a question into a closed question by giving a response such as, "It's good, no issues". In recognizing this, whilst gauging the atmosphere of the interview, the interviewer should be able to shift the impetus back, and ask a follow-up question such as, "Could you give an example of something you were happy with?"

A feedback interview conversation is a relationship tool and a branding experience for the firm and attention should be given to the flow and atmosphere of the interaction. On that basis, it is advisable to consider the timing of these more challenging questions. Asking such a question at the beginning of an interview can influence the course and the mood of the remainder of the discussion, so more potentially sensitive questions should come later in the discussion.

CASE STUDY

Case Study

During a client feedback interview scheduled with a CFO at an important "Top 50" client, they unexpectedly bring along the CEO to the meeting. Through the course of the regular questions, the tone of their responses indicates there is a problem.

The interviewer decides to bypass some questions and adopt a more challenging line of questioning in order to try to elicit the feedback the CEO wants to give. The CEO responds by saying that they are very unhappy with the service of one of the firm's partners and do not intend to give them any future work. They add that if it was not for the strength of their overall relationship, they would have changed firms already.

The interviewer is able to swiftly communicate this with the firm's relationship team and management, and action is taken to understand the issue and make changes to the client team. Through the feedback interview, and asking challenging questions, the firm is able to identify a major concern and client "flight risk", which would otherwise have been missed.

Months later, the CEO indicates that without the feedback interview, they would have simply given mid-level feedback, but in the background they would have put in place actions to change law firms in the near future.

Go "off piste" when given the invitation

In addition to asking more challenging questions, another technique that is likely to yield more valuable intelligence is to look for opportunities to expand on a response if there are indicators that there is more information to gather. Going "off piste", when appropriate, can open up a conversation and unlock information that may have gone undiscovered when navigating through the "surface" questions.

Case Study

A hypothetical scenario could go something like this:

Interviewer: Does Z & Co understand your business well?
Client: I think overall your knowledge of our business is strong. In general, the lawyers working for us know us and the market very well. We do, however, work with so many different lawyers at Z & Co.

I understand, yes. And what would you say about the firm's quality of legal advice?
It is difficult to say. I think Z & Co definitely meets our needs. When we need assistance then we get assistance from Z & Co.

OK, that's good to hear. Can you say a little more? It sounds like there is maybe something we could improve on.
It's normally great, excellent in fact. Other times it is not as good.

Interesting. Can you give an example?
On one occasion, we received some advice on X legislation and I was not that impressed and it became expensive. It was OK, there was nothing

wrong with it, but it wasn't very practical advice and it didn't really cover our needs. But it could have been our fault, the way we communicated it. We were so busy.

Thank you. Can I ask, did you give any feedback at the time?
No, like I say, we were very busy, and there was nothing specifically wrong with the advice.

By observing the responses and the tone, the interviewer was able to expand on the client's initial response. The client was satisfied overall and was initially hesitant to share more detailed feedback, but by asking two follow-up questions related to the topic of quality, the interviewer gained more valuable feedback. Even though the client tried to soften the feedback by taking responsibility for the issue, communicating the issue can help improve service delivery.

Strong reflective listening is very important. Interviewers need to be flexible in their questioning technique and not be so focused on the order of questions to the detriment of gaining valuable insights. It is also advisable to not become overburdened by recording notes so that you have sufficient capacity to listen closely to the answers that are given. This could mean bringing an additional person into the meeting in order to record responses in more detail, or it could be that you choose to record the interview, which should always be requested at some stage prior to the interview.

Giving the interviewee and the response greater attention ensures that the conversation flows more naturally and creates a more comfortable atmosphere that can often be conducive to more frank responses. It allows you to better identify opportunities for follow-up questions that can provide richer and more useful insights for the firm.

Ask the "hard" clients

As well as asking the hard questions, it is important to look carefully beyond the firm's top earning, institutionalized clients, with which the footprint is likely to be large and the relationship especially strong. Internal resistance to proposed feedback conversations tends to be significantly less for such clients, which should be telling in itself. These are clients deemed "safe" enough for feedback to be gathered from.

You can use a range of criteria to identify and target groups that might give you more valuable and actionable feedback. For example, criteria could include clients with a minor ongoing relationship but the existence of a major opportunity and spend, significant firm growth and increasing needs, and decrease in fees below a certain threshold despite continuing outside legal spend.

Have the right person asking the questions

Client feedback is a research exercise, independent of client relationship management. A client feedback interview should not replace a periodic client–partner meeting; they should be complementary, but they are separate discussions with different objectives. Research requires an objective approach, which generally means that interviews are best be carried out by someone independent of the relationship. When these interviewers are well briefed, they are in the optimal position to gather the most useful feedback. They also have a well-developed process and methodology to record feedback accurately and consistently, circulate it appropriately, and ensure follow-up.

These independent interviewers can either be third parties or internal staff, typically in a client development or business development department. These individuals should be adept in interviewing techniques so that they can, for example, skillfully handle negative feedback, avoid biased questions, and use appropriate probing questions to identify richer intelligence.

However you do it, make sure you act on the feedback

Regardless of your approach to obtaining client feedback, it is imperative that you always follow-up with clients if there is actionable feedback. Ninety percent of the time, there will be some follow-up actions that come out of a feedback interview. Failure to follow-up is not only a missed opportunity to make changes that can improve your firm. Far more dangerously, it can be detrimental to the relationship, more so than not asking for feedback at all. The client may think that there was no purpose in providing feedback and that they have wasted their time. By taking a proactive response to the feedback, you can solidify a trusted relationship with your clients, create connections to new opportunities, and adapt your service to their feedback.

Conclusion

When efficiently executed, a client feedback program can help firms gain valuable insight into their clients' opinions on the legal services provided, and much more. Posing the right questions that can elicit detailed and actionable intelligence and adopting a flexible interviewing style that focuses on reflective listening can provide valuable insights into how to improve the client experience. If firms follow through on the feedback, they are likely to experience an increase in client retention, in the number of new clients, and a rise in revenue.

References

1. https://bti-consulting.squarespace.com/bticlientfeedbackprograms

Chapter 3:

Cultural shift or cultural shove? The challenges of the client journey in the post-pandemic era

By Yolanda Cartusciello, partner, PP&C Consulting

A few weeks ago, I read an article[1] in which a prominent chief legal officer of a leading investment bank was positing that it will be difficult for law firms to train and mentor their young lawyers to perform at the level required if they did not return to physical offices full-time. In any event, he concluded, that investment bank would not accommodate Zoom meeting requests.

I have a 22-year-old daughter. When she was in pre-school, she made a best friend who moved away to California before grade school began. My daughter and her BFF managed to stay in contact throughout their lives, partially through the efforts of we parents who worked to get them together in-person when we could, but mostly through the magic of technology – Skype, FaceTime, Facebook, texting, you name it – they used it from first grade through high school and college. On the few occasions when they are in the same room, it seems as if they have been together every day. They have been physically apart practically all of their lives, but the closeness that they share is undeniable.

After my daughter graduated, she worked on the presidential campaign for Wisconsin. Notice that I did not say "in Wisconsin"; in point of fact, she never stepped foot in Wisconsin during the entire campaign. Because she was home, I had the privilege of hearing (eavesdropping, perhaps, is more accurate) meetings run by leaders virtually, and observed how well a remote team could work with a common cause. However, I thought, this can't be sustained in the long-run – after all, a campaign is finite and how much did she really have to learn to be able to contribute meaningfully to virtual field organizing. Now she is on her second job since graduation at a real live company, which is completely virtual. No office; no brick-and-mortar presence. It's not a law firm, but it's also not a simple position to master – it requires the development of relationships, rapport, and expertise. Yesterday I listened (again, eavesdropped on) a virtual retreat her company ran during the day. At one point they had a scavenger hunt and she was running around the house completely entrenched in both the exercise and the spirit of it all. I watch her work sometimes, amazed at her ability to do this all virtually.

I am not like my daughter. I crave the personal connection and believe I learn best at the elbow of others. So when the CLO stated, "individual lawyers learn and perform best, and collectively deliver the best results, when they are together," I understood where he was coming from. Since making that statement, many articles, responses, and challenges have been made to his assertion that law firms need to resume in-person work. Some point to the ability of the digital native generation (like my daughter) to develop real, lasting, and effective relationships, esprit de corps and work habits remotely. Some would look at that very example of my daughter and her best friend and point out that it began with an in-person relationship. Few would argue that there may be a generational difference in the learning styles and abilities of the digital natives to not only survive, but thrive, in virtual work arrangements.

And yet, in perhaps the most important respect, most of what the CLO and respondents have said is beside the point – except for the following two statements: 1) "It is now clear to me that a hybrid meeting of live participants and Zoom participants is challenging at best," and 2) "As a general rule, we will not be accommodating Zoom participation in critical meetings". While the fears the CLO expressed and the rationale for believing lawyers needed to be back at their desks are interesting, the first statement is based upon actual concrete experience and the second is a decree based upon that experience. This is a result of the recent *client journey* this CLO has experienced and continues to experience (negatively) in dealing with outside lawyers. We can argue all we want as to whether his prescription to solve the issue (e.g. getting everyone back to the office) is appropriate, fair, realistic, beyond his purview, etc.; no one can argue that he does not like the experience of hybrid meetings and on one is in a position to tell him he need run those meetings differently than he prefers… unless (well let's save that "unless" until a bit further in our discussion).

Client journeys in the pandemic and beyond

Much has been written (including by me)[2] on the subject of client journeys over the past five years, but all of that theoretical discussion came into sharp relief throughout the pandemic as clients desperately needed firms not only to help them navigate the business challenges they were facing, but also the reality of trying to run businesses and maintain and build remote relationships with their lawyers.

For the uninitiated, the definition of a client journey is simply the steps a client takes to get from Point A to Point B. Some of those steps include working with your law firm; some don't. While some of those steps are beyond the control of a law firm, at PP&C Consulting, we have found through our extensive client interviews that those firms and lawyers that focused on making the entire journey as smooth as possible for their clients provided a superior experience and enjoyed more loyal clients as a result. Simple enough in theory, but complicated immensely when, after the pandemic began, Point B was often a moving target, and frankly, disappeared completely for many clients. The paradox is that the more unclear this journey became, the more clients relied on law firms, organizations built on following precedent, to help them through it.

What the clients told us

At PP&C, a large portion of our work comes in the form of conducting client interviews on behalf of law firms. We've spoken to hundreds of clients in the past five years, and while the specifics of the relationships can have different contours, the overall trends point to unsurprising expectations of their outside lawyers across all clients. These include:

- Critical analysis;
- Pragmatic business advice;
- Efficient and cost-effective services;
- Swift turnarounds;
- Technological savvy;
- Unwavering attention to detail; and
- A deep and nuanced understanding of the client's business and risk tolerance.

We also interviewed over 100 clients for various law firms during the last 15 months[3] and found that the one theme that dominated the feedback once the pandemic disruptions began was the *quality of the relationship*. All other factors became subordinate components of the overriding relationship.

It was clear from our interviews that although "Point B" was often elusive, those firms that focused on trying to lessen the impact of the circumstances largely upon everyone's control – doing their best to hack through the wilderness of the unknown, working with clients on payment terms, finding ways to deliver high levels of service remotely, providing real-time specific advice, providing educational opportunities for free, mastering the basics of virtual interactions – were appreciated more than law firms realized and have positioned themselves to be rewarded in the future with deeper loyalty and expanded relationships and mandates.

Conversely, those firms that either did not meet the moment or imposed their own interpretations of what they believed clients wanted rather than listening to clients' needs, received pointed criticism and have ground to make up in order to shore up the relationship.

Interestingly, those clients that thought their lawyers were investing in the relationship were quick to excuse their outside lawyers for bumps in technology, disruptions in document delivery, and other issues that normally did not occur pre-pandemic. There was a clear and stated amount of leeway about Zoom and WebEx and the problems associated with virtual meetings because, "after all" as one client put it "we're all dealing with this – I can't fault them for not being perfect on this dimension when I never expected it before. And when we aren't good at it either. We're learning together."

That leeway was only offered to those firms that had already established a strong track record of performance on behalf of the client.

The shift versus the shove

What was also clear from the interviews is that there was a real split between those clients who welcomed the evolution of the virtual meeting, working from home, and other accommodations into a regular part of their working relationship with their firms and others who were eager to get back to what they called "normal". It would be easier if we could report that the dichotomy lined up evenly by age or by physical distance between the clients and their outside lawyers, or any number of other criteria – but it did not. We found clients of all ages, genders, sizes, etc., on either side of the argument.

These results should not surprise anyone who has spent time thinking about the client experience and journey. Remember, first and foremost, stop thinking about clients as organizations; we need to view them as people trying to serve their organizations under stressful circumstances. As always, people come in all types of personalities and have different needs depending upon a large set of criteria. The problem occurs when we all assume that there has been a general permanent shift in the way all people want law firms to deliver legal advice and services. At the start and throughout the pandemic, client alerts and CLEs abound; everyone was on Zoom or WebEx; pets were often spotted in the background; hard copy originals could not easily be produced. There are people who have spent their entire careers commuting and really enjoy being in an office setting. Couple that with the extraordinary challenges of sheltering in place for months under fear of illness. Is it no wonder that some clients felt more like they were getting shoved into a new paradigm? Is it really surprising that no matter how well their law firms performed, some of them want to get as far away from that experience as possible?

That "shove" phenomenon was felt on the law firm side as well. Professionals who long believed (as I did) that the best learning is that which takes place in-person, were challenged to find ways to not only maintain but develop and strengthen ties in a purely virtual manner. Some clients told us that outside lawyers even expressed exasperation and apologized for the constant reliance on technology and the like. Even without such prompting, however, some clients expressed their own desires to reduce their reliance on technology and new forms of collaboration. Yes, as mentioned, there were others who absolutely thrived in the new paradigm. And here is where the art of client journey management can come into play.

Client journey management

In a post-pandemic environment, competition for legal work is likely to get even more intense. Many clients told me their legal budgets were slashed during the pandemic and their CEOs are not keen to restore those budgets to pre-pandemic levels. This means firms need to find even more creative ways to not only deliver legal advice and services more efficiently, but also provide clients with a positive experience that engenders loyalty. Alas, there are hundreds of firms with competence, expertise, specialization, and – most importantly – capacity.

To complicate the situation further, every law firm is focused on providing an expanded set of services to their current clients. Firms that have developed strategies around expanding current client relationships need to improve not only individual matter-level experiences, but experiences for those clients that need more than one type of work from your firm. Can you say with confidence that those experiences are consistent for your clients across practices, industries, and geographies?

Client journey mapping

Today, more than ever, differentiating the client experience becomes a critical component of a law firm's success, and client journey mapping is an effective tool in helping firms differentiate that experience.

While client journey mapping may be new to law firms, this technique has been used successfully by corporations across industries and around the world. Consumer product and B2C organizations such as Amazon, Apple, and Disney, as well as B2B and consulting firms such as IBM and McKinsey, have focused on the client journey as a way of improving and distinguishing the client experience.

At PP&C Consulting, we've translated and adapted this technique for the law firm environment. Our experience using the PP&C Consulting client journey mapping technique with law firm practice and industry groups, as well as in business development training programs, has helped lawyers and firms better understand the experiences they deliver and how those experiences might be improved.

What is it?

The definition of a client journey map is a visual representation of the steps and perceptions that a specific client goes through over a period of time to accomplish a *specific* goal that may include some interactions with your organization. The map helps identify how the client views an organization by putting interactions in the context of the client's broader goals, objectives, and activities.

Client journey mapping is an effective tool to view the client experience at a granular level because it allows for more precise diagnosis, invites more specific reengineering that may include areas not normally addressed by other diagnostic tools, and helps identify the stages at which problems surface, as well as the stages of origination. It also helps identify the bright spots – all the places where the firm is performing well – and should be replicated elsewhere. (For a more in-depth discussion and explanation of client journey mapping, see *Innovations in Client Experience*, Ark Publishing, 2018.)

Journey mapping works because it helps to identify both specific and more general problems across the entire relationship. This journey information is critical to a law firm's success because it ensures money and resources are allocated to the appropriate areas, while also giving the firm a deeper understanding of what their clients really need from them over the long haul.

In addition to the specific client-by-client benefits, client journey mapping exercises allow firms to enjoy more long-term benefits.

Inject client thinking into the client journey design process

Involving clients in helping to design the experience is a new concept to firms at best. Clients regularly tell us that they would happily work with their firms to map out their matters at the beginning of an assignment. Yet, we see little evidence that firms are embracing the opportunity. Those firms that do so are enjoying the benefits of a marketing advantage and a more satisfied and loyal client base. We believe a major reason for this failing is that too many firms are employing a top-down edict to become more efficient and effective, but in an inward-facing manner that allows for little client input or team-based solution development. Research suggests that organizations that share client feedback broadly and involve clients in designing their journeys are considered more empathetic, receive more word-of-mouth recommendations, and enjoy higher client retention rates.

Identify new client needs and services

While many organizations that engage in client journey mapping focus on identifying and addressing issues and challenges, the exercise can also be used to uncover unmet client needs and the possible development of new services and leads. It is unlikely that such needs will be uncovered by creating one journey map; however, journey mapping across similar clients may expose opportunities that were otherwise hidden.

Provide management committees with a powerful governance tool

As a business decision-making tool, client journey maps bring clients' needs and expectations to the forefront of the conversation. They help you identify the most important moments in their journey, understand how your firm is delivering on those key needs and expectations, and prioritize investment in client experience improvement projects to drive growth. Intimate knowledge of your client's views and expectations can be a powerful antidote for management committees that need to tamp down unnecessary spending of either time or money on activities that do not contribute to driving growth.

Client journey mapping is a powerful tool for change. When employed correctly with proper preparation and follow-up, it will provide long-lasting benefits to your firm and clients alike.

Conclusion

So let's get back to our friend, the chief legal officer. How exactly do we get him to come around to the idea of incorporating Zoom more regularly into his interactions with outside law firms? Should we even try? First and foremost, listen to him. He did state a hybrid approach would not be tolerated for "critical" meetings, which means that there is some latitude there for other types of meetings. Find out from him, specifically, what didn't work – what isn't working – in those hybrid meetings. See if you can develop a method for addressing his concerns – slowly – and only in the non-critical meetings. Ask yourself why you need to bring him along (e.g. will he actually have a better set of lawyers working with him if he allows for flexibility?). Delight him with an experience that makes him less likely to view the hybrid approach as one he can't tolerate. But most importantly, don't shove if he's not interested in the shift.

References

1. "Morgan Stanley Top Lawyer Demands Law Firms Return to Office (2)", Brian Baxter, Bloomberg Business of Law https://news.bloomberglaw.com/business-and-practice/morgan-stanleys-legal-chief-wants-law-firms-back-in-the-office
2. "If You Want Lawyers to do a Better Job for You, Tell Them a Story", Yolanda Cartusciello, *Legal 500 Magazine*, November 2018 www.legal500.com/fivehundred-magazine/career-corner/if-you-want-lawyers-to-do-a-better-job-for-you-tell-them-a-story/
3. "That's Great, But Let's Talk About the Client (Perspective)", Yolanda Cartusciello, September 2016, Bloomberg Business of Law https://news.bloomberglaw.com/business-and-practice/thats-great-but-lets-talk-about-the-client-perspective/

Chapter 4:
Client journey mapping as a source of sustainable competitive advantage

By Andrew Hedley, Hedley Consulting

Client journey mapping is becoming *de rigueur* as leading firms seek ways to carve sustainable competitive advantage and bring clarity to their market positioning with increasingly discerning clients. This chapter sets out the strategic rationale for client journey mapping and provides pointers for law firm leaders to consider when introducing the techniques to their firm within a wider business development strategy.

Setting the strategic context: what client journey mapping is and why it matters

The nature of the relationship between the law firm and its clients has changed irrevocably at every level of the market. Put simply, clients want their legal services delivered better, faster, and cheaper. The balance of power has shifted with more change discerning to perceptive and sophisticated client decision-making, meaning that a basis for competitive differentiation is essential if firms are not to be drawn into unsustainable price-driven warfare.

However, a meaningful differentiation strategy is both challenging to develop and difficult to maintain. Within their respective weight classes, firms cannot differentiate on technical skills. They and their competitors are filled with lawyers of comparable ability (skills which in any event few clients are able to discern and evaluate) and consequently law firm strategies tend to be built on a platform of client intimacy. At its core, this means understanding current and future client needs to design a service model that meets these in a way that delivers higher value and increases trust. Central to this strategic approach is the design and consistent delivery of a client experience that is integrated, responsive, and appropriate at every client touchpoint. To create such a differentiation strategy requires developing a deep understanding of how a client feels during and after a service interaction.

A huge challenge for firms with a strategy based on client intimacy or centricity is that they are generally structured based on functional silos such as legal practice and business services departments. This structure manifests itself negatively to clients when they are passed from function to function during the delivery of their services, over the life of a matter or transaction. The same silos can also present significant obstacles to overcome when firms seek to implement service improvement initiatives or to act on feedback from client service reviews or listening programs.

When a firm's management hierarchy is based around functional teams, the challenge will always be to find ways to make effective change happen that reflect the way clients want to experience working with the firm; ideally, this will be a single seamless journey across all touchpoints through the entirety of their interaction with the firm. This should start with the initial "brand promises" communicated in advance of the client engaging the firm all the way through to post-transaction reviews and beyond to create an annuity relationship of repeat engagements. Of course, a brand promise sets expectations that then become the benchmark against which brand experience is measured. Indeed, it is the gap between brand promise and brand experience that will often be the root cause of client dissatisfaction. The dangers of over-promising and under-delivering are manifest.

One approach to understand and overcome these barriers is to consider the total client journey and design a service experience firmly rooted in this. This approach seeks to map the entire client experience across all touchpoints in order to align the experience that the client would wish to receive (for the price they are prepared to pay) and the experience that the firm aims to provide (at a profitable price point).

There is also a weighting factor to consider since all touchpoints will not be of the same importance to the client. It is important to understand the client's perspective and which touchpoints on the client journey are most critical in driving loyalty and repeat purchases.

It will also be vital to build a comprehensive understanding of the "moments of truth" where the desired client experience and the one that is actually received diverge, to understand how this has occurred and to ensure that rectifying actions are put in place in a focused way. The Servqual model, which is very helpful in making this assessment, is explained later in this chapter.

Client journey mapping as an integrative process

Put simply, client journey mapping is a technique for charting (generally in a visual format) the client's interaction with the business. It can be used in two ways – to map the journey of an external or internal client. From an internal client perspective, for example, the way in which a business support department services its internal client-facing departments would be a valid use of this methodology.

While, for the purposes of this chapter, we will primarily be considering the external client journey, it is crucial to recognize that the internal processes of any firm will have an impact on this and play a major role in shaping the experience the client has at the service interface.

This interplay can be better understood through the application of Service Blueprinting. This is a concept that was first explored by Lynn Shostack in *Harvard Business Review* in 1984.[1] Service blueprinting provides a framework to allow any service process to be segmented, analyzed, and opportunities for improvement and innovation evaluated. The blueprint comprises five components, illustrated in Figure 1, which may be thought of in a law firm context as comprising the following.

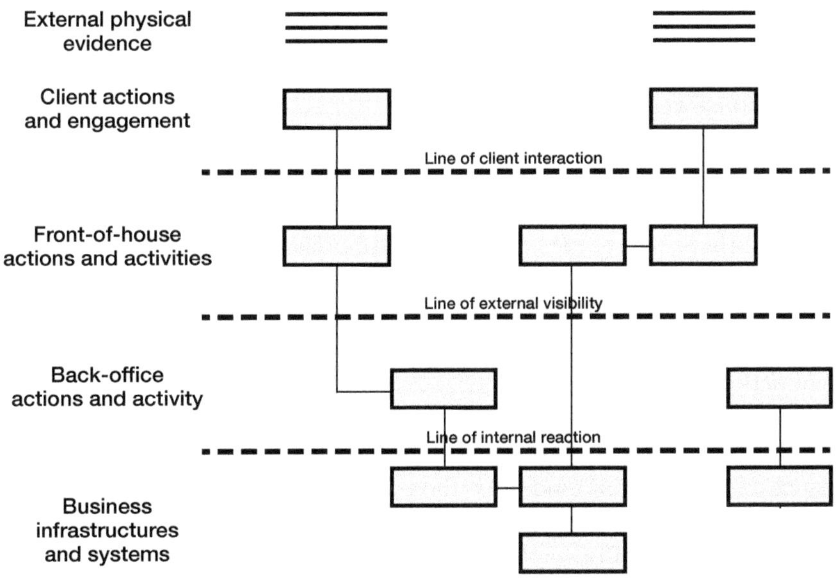

Figure 1: Service blueprinting concept organogram.

Business infrastructure and systems

Firstly, there are the business infrastructure and systems that are central to the delivery of the service. The innovative use of information technology to support the delivery of legal services has been a feature of many firms seen to be mold-breaking. Such approaches can deliver improved quality of client experience and the reduction of recurring costs, the holy grail of service innovation and client journey enhancement. What seems clear is that law firms in the future will have fewer people and more computers. This is not to say that human interactions will not retain a crucial part in many legal service transactions but rather that non-client facing, or process-rich, elements will be increasingly delivered by machines rather than people. Examples of these non-human interactions that shape the service experience would include the use of client portals, collaboration tools for document sharing, and providing direct access to financial information.

Back-office actions and activity

The back-office actions and activity tier relates to staff (both business support and legal service delivery) who do not normally have face-to-face client interactions. Nonetheless they have a significant role in shaping the current service experience as well as providing opportunities for future service innovation.

Front-of-house actions and activity

The activity and actions of staff who do have face-to-face client interactions as part of their normal routine is a further layer of the blueprint. For the avoidance of doubt, in addition to client-facing lawyers this might include, amongst others, secretaries, IT staff, telephonists, receptionists, catering personnel, and others who directly shape the client experience and are a central part of the client journey map.

Client actions and engagement

The fourth aspect of the blueprint is concerned with the actions required of the client in order to engage with the firm. It is a universal truism that businesses that do well tend to be those that are easy to do business with. It can be remarkably hard to interact with many law firms when viewed through the lens of a busy client. There are significant client journey and service enhancement opportunities to be had in this component of the blueprint.

External physical evidence

Finally, there are the physical evidence elements of service that need to be considered. These include, for example, the firm's marketing, premises, accessibility, and market positioning. Relentlessly finding new ways of reaching out to prospective clients and engaging more fully with existing ones as part of their client journey map will be a feature of successful law firms in the future.

Each component presents opportunities for improvement, to do things in a way that is more client-centric and that improves the client brand experience. Furthermore, the relationship and interaction between components provides a further dimension for those seeking opportunities for competitive advantage. Indeed, it will often be the case that it is by creating service strategies that cross the component boundaries that solutions are produced that are difficult for competitors to imitate quickly or closely. Client journey maps allow these synergies to be identified and capitalized upon.

Understanding touchpoints: necessary but not sufficient

For clients and prospects, perceptions and reputation are created and built (or destroyed) at their touchpoints with the business. These touchpoints are varied and far-ranging, encompassing highly-managed interactions through to the more run-of-the-mill experiences of contact with the firm. At the one extreme they are tightly controlled (for example, corporate literature, seminars, hospitality, newsletters, and bulletins), while at the other they are concerned with the day-to-day experiences gained in the working environment. This will range from the mundane, such as telephone responsiveness and manner, to insightful symbols like the commerciality of the firm's approach, the clarity of its business communications, and the way in which projects are delivered to time and budget (or not as the case may be!).

Creating a touchpoint map can be a very powerful way in which to better understand and assess the client experience that the firm delivers and where gaps or inconsistences occur. The creation of the map involves the identification of every interaction that clients have with the firm, what this experience is, and how it shapes the client's perception of the business. This understanding allows actions to be put in place to rectify shortcomings or service failures in a structured way.

It is relevant to point out that interactions may be real or virtual. For example, an important touchpoint to be managed is the firm's marketing communications presence, which may be virtual through websites and social media as well as physical in the shape of communications collateral. Many "brand promises" are made at this stage and expectations set about "what it will be like" at both a practical and emotional level to work with the firm. These assertions set a framework of expectations against which future experiences and service delivery is judged.

A simplified example of a touchpoint map is shown in Figure 2 overleaf. It serves to illustrate an important issue that firms must resolve. In considering the numerous client touchpoints with the business, there is one obvious line of demarcation – those that are controlled and administered by the formal management team versus those that fall to the client-facing lawyer. In the former category will typically sit touchpoints in the marketing presence and physical evidence categories. In the latter will be face-to-face interaction. Bridging the two will be a range of touchpoints, for example those related to the application of house style.

It is a truism that, in most firms, the level of consistency of experience is greater in the areas controlled from the center than those that are left to the relative discretion of the individual. It is also important to note that one should not confuse consistency and quality *per se*. One would generally want the client experience to be both consistent and of a high quality (one might use the term "appropriate quality" in arenas that are more price-driven). However, it is also fair to point out that an inconsistent approach does not necessarily mean one of low quality (although it will certainly suggest variable quality). The key point for the leader tasked with developing a service strategy is that such inconsistency is not compatible with building a robust client experience and delivery model.

Creating a touchpoint map, valuable as it may be, does not tell the whole story. As Nicholas Maechler, Kevin Nehler, and Robert Park of McKinsey & Company point out:

> *"To maximise [client] satisfaction, [firms] have long emphasized touchpoints. But doing so can divert attention from the more important issue: the [client's] end-to-end journey."*[2]

They make a compelling argument that simply focusing on individual touchpoints, while undoubtedly of value, is not striking at the core issue. The touchpoint map is necessary but not sufficient. From a client defection perspective, they argue that "what was driving them out of the door was something the [firm] wasn't examining or managing – the [client's] cumulative experience across multiple touchpoints, multiple channels, and over time."

This is why an analysis based on a deeper understanding of the entire client journey offers a more compelling and effective approach.

Stages of the client journey

When done well, journey mapping depicts each point of a client's interface with the firm and provides a deeper and more comprehensive

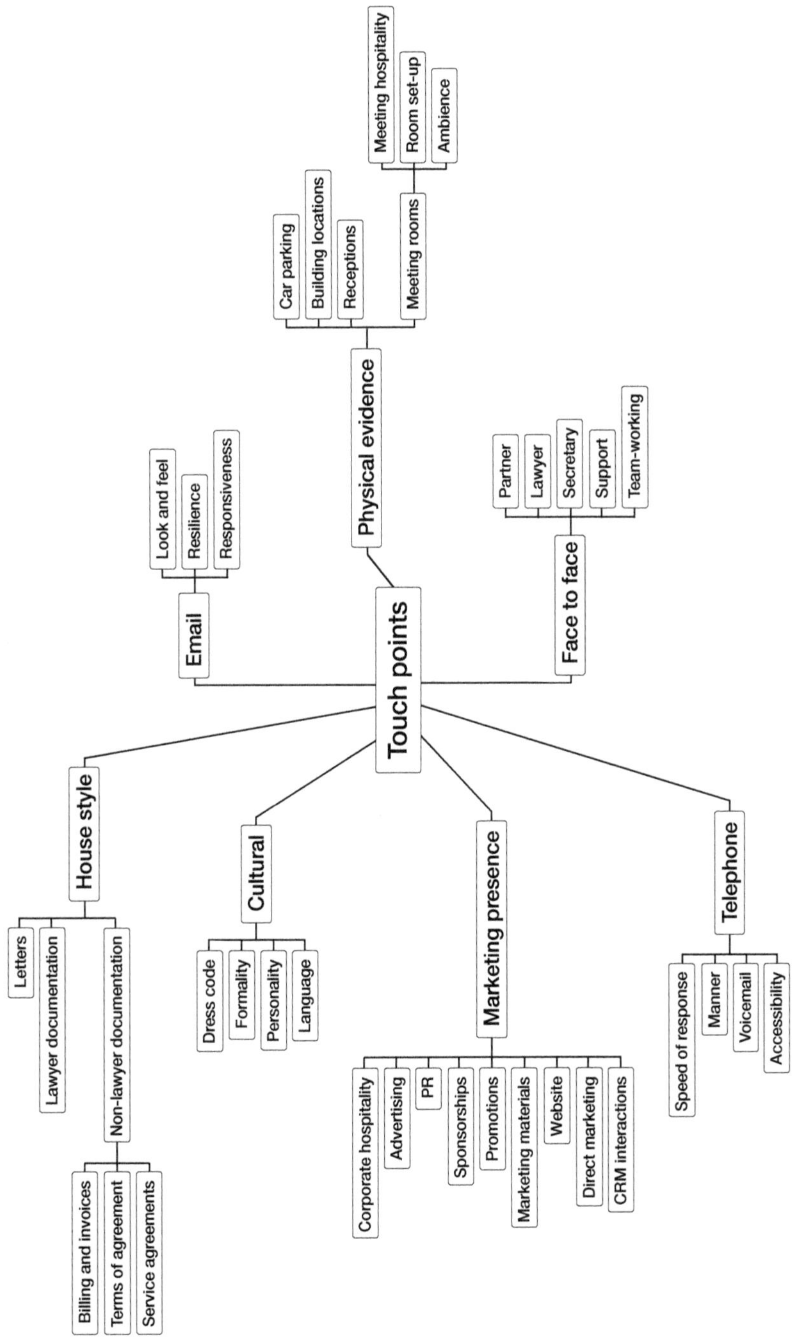

Figure 2: Touchpoint map.

understanding of what the client experiences as they engage with the firm. This engagement can be looked at through a number of lenses – legal department service lines, business support services, individual interactions, and the firm as a whole.

In unpacking the client journey it is helpful to consider the timeline that is typically followed in order to understand better the charting of the route map. There are many different frameworks that can be used to map this journey but they generally share three common components in seeking to understand what the client is experiencing (and what the client desires) before, during, and after the engagement.

Pre-engagement phase

Understanding the client journey that leads to the engagement of the firm is critical in building a more successful and efficient sales pipeline. By unearthing the reasons why a client chooses to contact one firm over another, it is possible to shape existing systems and design new ones to maximize the chances of success. Finding ways to "move the dial" only a few notches to generate incremental improvements in pre-engagement touchpoints can lead to dramatic up-ticks in the levels of activity that the firm experiences.

Engagement phase

At the first stage of any engagement there is a client onboarding process – this will be more in-depth (and potentially complex) for a new client but still necessary for an annuity relationship. This is the point at which standards are set, interfaces agreed, and relationships established. At this point journey mapping will aggregate a number of potentially discrete streams of activity – it would not be uncommon, for example, for finance, knowledge management, account management, learning and development, and of course the relevant practice groups to be part of the overall journey map.

By developing client personas, firms are able to enhance the services that they already deliver as well as anticipating the future needs of a fast-moving client base. By so doing the firm is able to illustrate that it is ahead of the curve, demonstrate segment leadership, and articulate a strongly differentiated offer. This serves to bolster the overall brand, reducing competitive threats, and allowing for more robust pricing. By anticipating needs better, improving collaboration both with clients and internally, it is possible to broaden and deepen client relationships, improve resilience, and build entry barriers against competitor firms.

Post-engagement phase

It is critical that the client journey mapping doesn't cease when the engagement ends. While the conduct of post-transaction or relationship reviews is now commonplace, it should not be thought that this is the summation of the client journey.

Indeed, post-matter engagement is crucial to building the sort of longer-term repeat-business annuity relationships that firms desire. The evidence is clear that time spent off the clock is highly valued and significantly influences future purchasing decisions.

For those firms whose work is of a more one-off transaction or occasional matter nature, the post-engagement journey is still important. Post-engagement activity secures future goodwill, ensuring that, when further needs arise, the firm is front of mind and the obvious choice. It also leverages the potential for referral from the satisfied client to its network.

Managing post-engagement touchpoints, building ongoing relationships, improving loyalty, and brand presence is a key part of the client journey map.

Using Servqual to understand and align brand promise with brand experience

In managing the client journey, it is vital to build a clear understanding of where service failures may occur. There are numerous interactions taking place between the firm and its clients as well as within the firm itself; failure at any one can lead to the desired service levels not being achieved and the firm more broadly being unable to operate in a consistent way.

To illustrate these interactions and potential sources of service quality failure, the diagram in Figure 3 overleaf sets out a model developed from Servqual theories by Hedley Consulting[3] to reflect the law firm context.

This model highlights the gaps that may exist in terms of how a service meets clients' needs or expectations, together with how well these gaps are understood and communicated within the firm. Taking each of these gaps in turn, it is possible to dissect, analyze, design, and better manage a firm's service quality processes and the impact on the overall client journey.

Gap 1: The difference between client expectations and perceptions of the service delivered

This is the point at which the rubber hits the road – where expectations and experience collide. However, while this may be the first point at which service failure is manifested, its gestation has been long-coming. It is an inevitable consequence of failures elsewhere in the service strategy and the planning of the client journey.

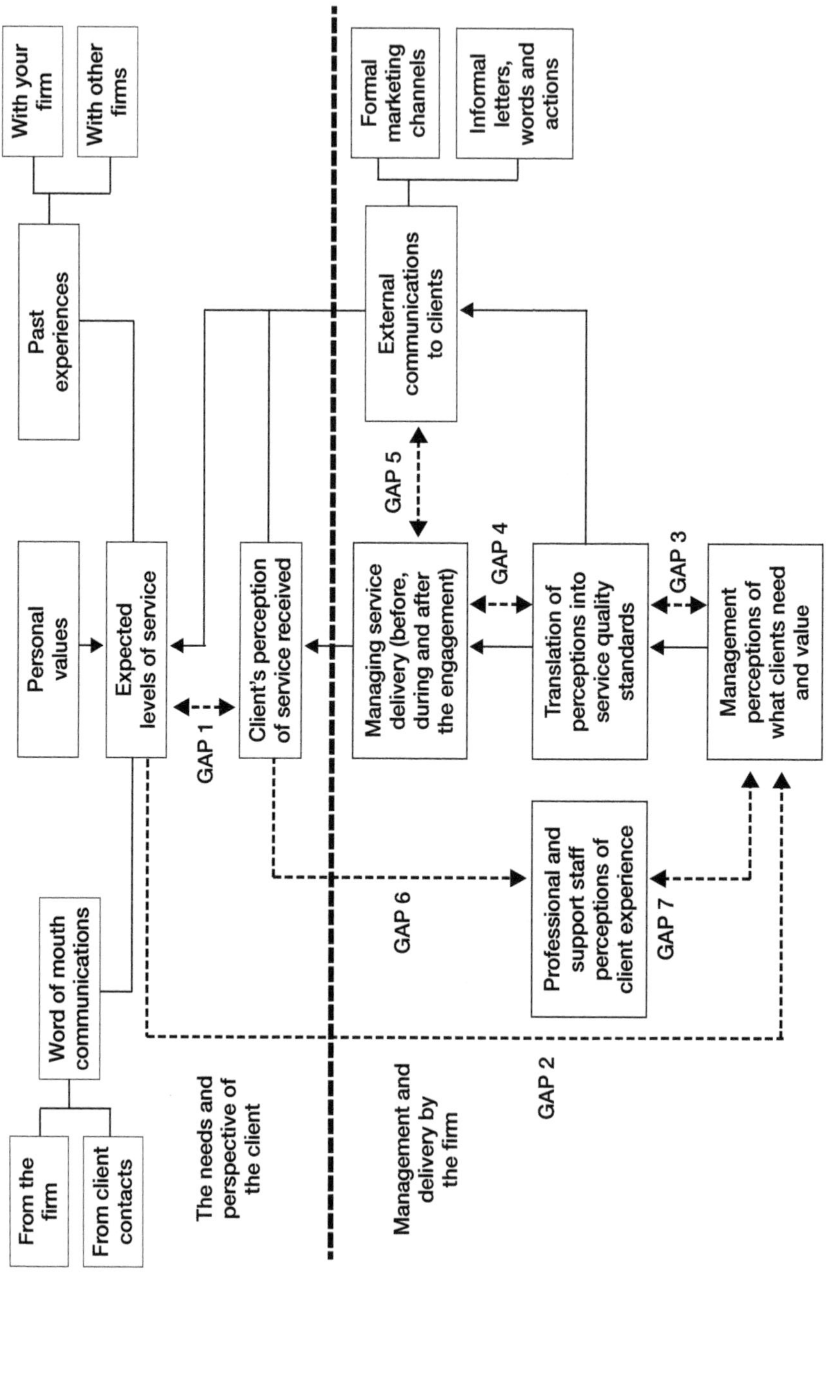

Figure 3: Possible client–firm service quality gaps.

This gap arises because of the discrepancy between the influences exerted from the client side and the shortfalls on the part of the law firm in delivering against them. Clients have a level of expected service that is shaped by their own needs (or standards), past experiences with the firm (or other firms perceived as being similar), and what they have heard "on the grapevine" or through word-of-mouth recommendation concerning the way in which the firm delivers its services. Taken together, this creates the yardstick by which their journey will be judged.

Gap 2: Clients' expectations versus the perceptions of the firm's management team

Management teams that do not invest in research (or do not take on board the results of the research that they commission) can find themselves out of kilter with fast-changing client expectations of service. In a dynamic environment, expectations shift constantly and the service innovation of last year becomes the norm of today.

Other issues seen at this point can be inadequate upwards communication within the firm, or too many layers of administration (and vested interests!) shielding or skewing information flows to the senior management team.

It is important to appreciate that a failure at this point has the potential to condemn the rest of the process to misalignment with client needs. Even perfect execution from this point will lead to a sub-optimal result if the objective being targeted is incorrect. The same effect can be tracked throughout the model – if the starting point is wrong, then the probability of arriving at the correct end point is low.

Gap 3: The ability of the management team to translate its perceptions into adequate service standards

If the management team cannot translate its perceptions of client needs into service standards that adequately reflect this and can be implemented within the business then the potential for an ultimate failure in the client journey increases significantly.

Furthermore, the management team needs to be truly committed to meeting its own service standards, ensuring that current clients' needs are fully met, as well as stretching resources to achieve those that are anticipated in the future. Without such commitment, there can be a perception that achieving the required service standards is unfeasible, or that there is slackness in setting stretching targets or insisting on high standards of consistency in delivery.

Gap 4: Managing service delivery (before, during, and after the engagement)

Failure here can happen for a number of reasons – lack of skills, resource shortages, poor technology support, poor team-working, and inadequate supervision, to name a few. For many law firms the operational aspects of service delivery are particularly challenging because they require professionals to conform to a standardized modus operandi. They also require those in management roles to acquire skills that do not form part of their professional training and that they often do not relish.

Gap 5: The actual delivery of the service versus expectations set by external communication

The classic error of over-promising and then under-delivering falls squarely into this area. By de-coupling external marketing communications from the firm's ability to deliver, a serious issue is potentially created. Too many firms base their external communications on "what the client wants to hear" without any grounding in the reality of the firm's ability to deliver against such expectations. Consequently, many firms say the same thing but few deliver on their promises.

Gap 6: The difference between client expectations and the perceptions of staff

If staff, at all levels, don't have a clear understanding of what service standards have been agreed, then it is unlikely that they will meet client expectations in an efficient way. Without clarity in these areas there is a possibility that the firm will over-perform (and carry the cost of so doing) in non-critical areas, only to underperform (and perhaps incur the penalty of client dissatisfaction) in a business-critical dimension.

Gap 7: The difference between the perceptions of staff and those of the management team

Unless internal communications and systems ensure that both groups have a clear and shared understanding of what is required in terms of service standards, expectations, and delivery, a shortfall will be inevitable.

Taking things forward

For those charged with the task of client journey mapping, there are a number of sources readily available that offer useful information and practical tools to assist with service design; for example the Service Design Tools website.[4] Such tools and methodologies can be invaluable in analyzing, shaping, planning, and delivering the hard-wiring and structures that will be required.

As well as putting in place the systems and processes to make the client journey central to the firm's service delivery strategy, it will also be important to mold cultural aspects so that "standing in the shoes of the client" is the norm. There is also a need for leadership and example-setting from the senior people in the firm. It is critical that desirable behaviors are driven through the business as well as strong resolve in dealing with those that are unacceptable.

Client journey mapping, together with the activity that flows from it, sits at the center of any client strategy. For those firms that prioritize client-centric approaches of this nature, there are significant opportunities to consistently deliver a level of client experience that is distinctive, valuable, and hard for competitors to imitate. These are key attributes of differentiation that in turn drives sustainable competitive advantage.

References

1. Shostack, G. L., "Designing Services that Deliver", *Harvard Business Review*, vol. 62, no. 1, January-February 1984. Subsequently developed further by others, for example in Bitner, Ostrom & Morgan, *Service Blueprinting: A Practical Technique for Service Innovation*, Centre for Services Leadership, Arizona State University, 2007, and Wilson, Zeithaml, Bitner & Gremler, *Services Marketing: Integrating Customers Focus Across the Firm* (2008).
2. Maechler, N., Nehler, K., and Park, R. "From touchpoints to journeys: seeing the world as customers do", McKinsey & Company, March 2016. See www.mckinsey.com/business-functions/marketing-and-sales/our-insights/from-touchpoints-to-journeys-seeing-the-world-as-customers-do.
3. www.hedleyconsulting.com/service-quality-reputation-management-strategy/
4. See www.servicedesigntools.org/.

Chapter 5:
Client loyalty – delivering exceptional client service

By David H. Freeman, JD, CEO of the David Freeman Consulting Group

"Do what you do so well that they will want to see it again and bring their friends."
Walt Disney

Lawyers can differentiate themselves in a number of ways, such as through the quality of their work product, how clients pay for the service, and the experience the client has working with their lawyer. In this chapter, we focus on maximizing the third factor – how to deliver superior levels of client service – as well as provide insights from a number of experts in the field.

Great service is not just a "nice-to-have" – there is a clear link between high levels of client service and financial rewards, as demonstrated by BTI Consulting Group's research showing that firms with consistently superior client service enjoy hourly rate premiums, higher profits per partner, and greater client retention.[1] For this section, we include insights from several experts in this field, including Jan Anne Dubin, CEO and founder at Jan Anne Dubin Consulting (and former head of North American business development for Baker & McKenzie, and former head of client relations at DLA Piper) and Adam Stock, head of legal operations and financial compliance at Worldcoin and former director of marketing and business development at Allen Matkins Leck Gamble Mallory & Natsis LLP.

Build long-term relationships

For a relationship to flow smoothly there should be synergy between the client and the attorney, who must work together as a team. True teaming – delivering to deadlines, being transparent, and upholding promises on both sides – is the essential currency of becoming a trusted advisor. Jan Anne Dubin, CEO and founder at Jan Anne Dubin Consulting, former head of North American business development for Baker & McKenzie, and former head of client relations at DLA Piper, is deeply focused on helping lawyers deliver higher levels of service, and one of her favorite books on the subject is *The Trusted Advisor.*[2] She explains:

> *"One of the main tenets of the book is that you must invest in the relationship and, quoting from the book, 'the deepest and most complete trusted advisor relationships (have) few boundaries [...], little separation between professional and personal issues. Both members of the relationship fully know about each other and understand the role the other plays in his or her life'. The book suggests we must place a higher value on the person than getting any single piece of work from that person, and by investing in the long-term relationship, it yields better results for everyone involved."*

Be highly responsive

One of the most frequently cited reasons why clients fire their lawyers is due to a lack of responsiveness. But that term – responsiveness – can mean many things to many people. According to Jan Anne, you must "provide client service that is tailored and unique to the needs and preferences of the specific client. It's critical to understand what your client values and manage yourself to those expectations. Don't make assumptions – the only way to know how is to ask them."

While it may be fine with some clients to return their calls by the end of the day, others may become livid if they don't hear back within the hour. Also, some clients will be impressed that you worked through the night to get their work done, while others may be offended that you didn't think they were important enough to fit into your regular workday and/or your tired "4am mind" is handling their critically important issues.

The lesson is, don't guess. Never presume to know exactly what people want. Every client has different needs and preferences, and every person inside an organization has their own set of expectations. The following are some examples of questions you might ask at the beginning of a relationship to learn more about how your clients define good service:

- What are your overall business goals?
- What have your favorite lawyers done for you, and what don't you like when working with outside lawyers?
- What is most important for you in a relationship with your lawyers?
- What does great service mean to you?
- How often would you like to hear from me?
- Do you prefer paper, email, text, or telephone?

- How can we make working together easy for you?
- How do you measure the success of a relationship with an outside lawyer?

Jan Anne comments, "When you listen to what the purchasers of legal services say about the client service they typically receive, they will tell you the bar is set fairly low. By applying some very simple techniques – listening and asking questions – you can truly differentiate yourself from most of your competitors."

The new math

The old school mindset of "Do a good job for a client, and that's all you'll need to build your book of business" is no longer viable. In today's over-saturated market, it's not enough to just deliver a technically good result. The fact is, sophisticated clients can choose from scores of highly qualified lawyers. To stand out, to own a higher priority position in the client's mind, you must do more. The new arithmetic for attracting, keeping, and growing clients can be stated as follows:

Good work + excellent experiences = more work.

A director of client development at an AM Law firm concurs:

> *"It's loud and clear, now, more than ever – clients no longer only want legal advice. They want someone who will look out for their business interests. To match these expectations, you should do more than just answer the legal question posed. Be proactive. Think about the client's business as though it were your own. Go beyond just being a lawyer and act as a business advisor, even if they haven't expressly asked for that level of service. In today's world, you have to make the experience of working with you and your firm an equally important part of the equation."*

This director adds that smaller firms may have an advantage in this area "due to the nimbleness that much larger firms don't have. Smaller firms are not as constrained by volumes of firm policies or numerous levels of management approval. They can make quick decisions, and if needed, can add bench strength quickly by partnering with other firms."

Along with being an advisor, make them feel like they're your most important client. How would you act if that were the case? Think of how you treat a best friend. You think about their needs, help without being asked, have fun, protect their back, stay in touch, make them feel safe, and share in joys and sorrows. All of these characteristics can translate to a client relationship. The following sections will demonstrate various approaches for delivering outstanding experiences to clients, prospects, and referral sources.

Get on their turf

A lawyer I know had one main client and spent every workday on site at the client's location. While this exact approach is not applicable for most outside lawyers, it illustrates a powerful way to know a client's operations, people, culture, needs, and internal politics. Being on-site positions you as one of them and makes you an indispensable part of the client's team. Some lawyers have a variation on this theme – for their best clients, they conduct "office hours" where they'll come on-site, say, once a month for a day, to do the client's work. The client gets the benefit of having the lawyer immediately available to pick their brain, and the lawyer becomes intimately involved in the business and meets more decision-makers.

Also, I've seen lawyers who offer to participate in clients' internal strategic planning meetings, whether live or remotely, to provide a fresh perspective into their planning discussions. One managing partner reported that not only did her client deeply appreciate her presence in these meetings, but she got three new pieces of work that she believed would not have come to her had she not been present in those sessions.

Another approach is to be proactive and offer your services (or those of another firm lawyer) when a client has a short-term need for in-house help – perhaps one of their lawyers is on maternity, they lose someone, or an issue arises that needs immediate support. Many heads of business development have seen success with this approach. One leader I spoke with states, "Lawyers I've worked with who have used this approach have received more work because the lawyer on-site kept their ears open for opportunities where we could help in other areas".

Jan Anne has a similar experience, highlighting the importance of getting close to your client. "A lawyer I knew would literally walk the halls of a large hotel company's legal department and come back with many new opportunities. It's a quick, easy way to learn about their challenges and pressures, which they might not share through a phone call."

Understand the client's business

One of the key pillars of client service is developing a strong understanding of their business and industry. In many law firms, a relatively small portion of clients are responsible for a high percentage of the revenue, so you should invest additional time on those key clients. Adam Stock, head of legal operations and financial compliance at Worldcoin and former director of marketing and business development at Allen Matkins Leck Gamble Mallory & Natsis LLP urges:

> *"You should be on top of what they want and need and know their issues. Make a proactive effort not only to focus the best minds in the firm on them, but also make sure your firm's best resources are available to serve them. Services provided by companies such as Thomson Reuters and LexisNexis allow you to get some pretty remarkable background on clients. Have a look at a client's legal history. You should also conduct a client review process – pick your top clients and have a discussion with management about client needs and industry needs. Build an action plan around that. The idea is very simple – most non-legal businesses stay close to their best clients and understand what they're buying. As an industry, law firms are generally not good at this – we don't spend time with our management teams determining what's important to clients and how we should respond. That must change."*

Monitor your clients' websites for news alerts, sign up for a clipping service that automatically sends you information on the client or industry, and do a Google search before conversing with clients in order to stay up-to-date with their business. You can also ask clients and prospects what they read, which allows you to stay up on their latest trends and issues. For public companies, listen to their earnings calls, which are open to the public and provide insight as to the company's current and future circumstances.

Client feedback

Loyal clients will go out of their way to make you successful, there is less chance of them leaving for another firm, and they are more likely to refer you to others for new business. If you can achieve client loyalty, the financial rewards for you and your firm can be very significant. You will also have much happier clients, so it is truly a win-win situation.

You must never take even your best clients for granted. In fact, if they're that good, it probably means other law firms are aggressively trying to woo them away from you. To protect against this poaching, you must always have your pulse on the quality of the relationship, which can be accomplished by asking for feedback. Asking for, and acting upon, client feedback is clearly one of the best techniques used by law firms today to protect and grow their most strategically important relationships.

One head of business development at a large firm pointed out another important factor to consider:

> *"Achieving average levels of client satisfaction is no longer enough. Clients are much more discerning now; they know they have control. What we're going for is client loyalty, based on higher levels of satisfaction. Start by talking to the client – learn about their needs and where their business is going."*

One of the great challenges is that stubborn population of partners who try to block access to strategically important clients. If the client is that critical to the firm, this simply can't be allowed. If leaders cannot convince or force them to do it, then perhaps use peer pressure – facilitate a partner-wide discussion of the vital importance of getting feedback for your A-list clients, name those clients, agree upon a feedback strategy, and get group commitment to hold each other accountable for getting it done. You should also discuss the consequences of not complying. The future of clients that are so important to the firm should not be left up to one person.

Visit top clients to receive feedback

Where possible, lawyers should regularly meet with clients at their location to learn how they feel about the level of service. Use the visit as an opportunity to meet other decisions-makers inside their organization. The visit itself can be a differentiator – I've often heard clients say that no lawyer has ever come on-site to visit them, and they appreciate the effort. Often the mere act of going on-site and asking for feedback can generate new opportunities.

Client service teams

Form a team around your most important clients. Include others who work with that client on a regular basis. Paralegals, secretaries, associates, partners – there are so many touches to a client, which means there can be many places where there can be service breaks, as well as new opportunities to serve them. You must cover them all. Make sure the client service team meets regularly to discuss:

- What is happening with their work;
- What is happening in their industry;
- Changes to personnel;
- Any service issues that have occurred; and
- Possible areas where we can serve other needs.

The feedback process

For feedback to be valuable, clients must feel comfortable being open and honest about their experiences. In many cases, the lawyer who does the work can ask questions in ways that allow the client to be candid. However, in situations where you believe the client may not be forthcoming speaking to the lawyer who does the work, it might be best to appoint a third party, whether it be another lawyer in the firm, an in-house marketing professional, or an external consultant.

Listen carefully for feedback about the service you provide. Look for areas of dissatisfaction and find out how these could be improved. You can also use the feedback process as an opportunity to address other questions that are critical to your relationship such as:

- How many other law firms are you using?
- Who are our key competitors?
- Why are you using these other firms instead of us?
- What are they doing that I am not?

Annual client meetings

By touching base with the client in a regular, defined way that is not specifically linked with ongoing matters, you create a space in which you can identify upcoming issues and new opportunities. These check-in meetings can cover issues including:

- What you did this year;
- What you charged the client;
- Fees billed and written down;
- Non-billable time invested;
- Overall satisfaction – what did they like, what should we do differently;
- What is going on in the client's company;
- What kind of challenges and projects they expect to have; and
- Other ways we can help.

One business development leader advises:

> *"This is a substantive meeting. It's not done over dinner, golf, or a ball game. You need to allow an hour or two for a meeting like this, depending on the*

size of the client – in some instances we've had a meeting go on all day. Listen to the client: find out where they're heading and what's on their mind. Don't use this meeting as an opportunity to sell. If the client opens the door for that kind of conversation, then it's fair game. Otherwise just listen, take notes, and come back to them later with a game plan for helping them."

End-of-matter reviews

If you don't have the resources to conduct a full client feedback program, instead carry out formal or informal end-of-matter reviews. Sit down with the client at the end of any major matter and gather feedback on the firm's performance.

End-of-matter reviews are far more effective if you can compare the feedback with objectives and expectations that were in place at the beginning of the matter. For this purpose, a pre-matter plan should be drawn up. Some key points to cover in the pre-matter plan might include:

- What do we plan to achieve with this project?
- What is the best way to communicate with you?
- How often?
- When do you want updates?

At the end-of-matter review, compare your performance against the pre-matter expectations. Consider scoring yourself in areas such as:

- Did we achieve the objectives?
- Did we achieve the ideal outcome?
- Did you get what you wanted?
- Did we do anything that disappointed or pleased you?

Mid-matter reviews

For major matters that span several months or years, conduct a mid-matter review. This avoids unpleasant surprises at the end of the matter and guards against frustrations that could have been avoided if addressed early on in the process.

Act on feedback

The single most important part of the feedback process is developing a plan based on the feedback, and then acting on that plan. Jan Anne explains,

"There is nothing more frustrating to a client than to take their time – waste their time – if the feedback is not going to be heeded and applied by the firm." Once you've created the plan, share your observations with the client, get their input, and develop a timeline for making any requested changes. This deepens the trust and connection, while bringing a level of accountability into the process. For your most important clients, appoint a "Watcher" – a senior leader who will track progress and hold people accountable for timely implementation of the plan.

Deliver added value

You need to remember you are both an attorney and counselor at law, and by using more of your counseling skills, you can become a more valuable, integral, and irreplaceable part of the client's team. Proactive, value-added counseling has many benefits:

- It demonstrates that you care and are looking out for their interests;
- It shows you understand the client's business and how it is affected by changes;
- It demonstrates that you are up-to-date with key issues in their industry; and
- You can make welcomed contact that might turn into new work.

ACC Value Challenge

One of the best resources for inside and outside lawyers to learn how to add value comes from the Association of Corporate Counsel through its ACC Value Challenge,[3] which is an initiative to "reconnect the value and the cost of legal services". Many people assume that, when a client mentions value or alternative fees, it's just a veiled way to request lower fees. While this may be true in some cases, it is not always the complete picture; the ACC Value Challenge presents a balanced view of what both clients and law firms want and need. By considering the needs of both parties in the relationship, the Value Challenge helps law firms take practical steps toward delivering greater value to clients rather than simply conceding discounts. Spending some time on the ACC Value Challenge website and learning various approaches for delivering added value might be one of the best investments you can make in your practice.

Work as a team

The beauty of the Value Challenge is that it provides a framework for engaging in a dialogue about how to serve the needs of both sides. Adam explains:

> *"In some situations, we may not be working as efficiently as possible. In other areas, due to our experience and skill, we can often save clients significant money by averting a lawsuit or spotting a potential risk. There are things we charge very little for that deliver huge value, and there are things we could do far more effectively. Using the format provided by the ACC Value Challenge, we can openly discuss how to make the engagement work better for everyone."*

Other techniques for delivering exceptional service

As a final note, consider the following:

- Anticipate their legal needs before they even ask;
- Prevent issues before they arise through training and reviews;
- Provide targeted updates on legal developments;
- Develop fee structures that deliver price certainty;
- Develop checklists to manage timelines and expectations;
- Offer on-site training;
- Give out home and cell numbers;
- Pick up your own phone;
- Create a succession plan;
- For larger clients, appoint a relationship manager;
- Build relationships with the client's staff;
- Make introductions to people they'd like to meet;
- Develop status reports and deliver them in a format they can send to their superiors;
- Develop an extranet where clients can see the status of their matters all in one place;
- Provide electronic copies of documents they can file internally;
- Understand their billing systems and adapt to their approaches;
- Help them (or family members) get jobs;

- Let them use your meeting rooms;
- Send letters praising their work to their superiors;
- Be an advocate for them inside your firm and find resources they need;
- Support their community service initiatives;
- For social functions, create family friendly events; and
- Learn how they are compensated and see if there are ways you can help them make more money.

References

1. See https://bticonsulting.com/client-feedback-programs, BTI Consulting Group, Wellesley, MA.
2. Maister, D., Green, C. and Galford, R. *The Trusted Advisor.* The Free Press, New York, 2000.
3. www.acc.com/services-initiatives/value-challenge

Chapter 6:

Defining, measuring, and delivering a stellar client service strategy

By Kim Carr, lead partner of the wills, probate, and lifetime planning department, FBC Manby Bowdler LLP

To be truly fit for a more competitive, customer-focused future, the modern law firm has to look and act very differently from the creature it was only a handful of years ago. For most organizations, the truth is that it's not an easy transformation to carry out. When we decided that our concept of "stellar service" was going to be at the heart of everything we did, we were embarking on a journey that was full of challenges, close self-examination, careful listening, and a need to be willing to change and adapt. Also, every single person in the firm had to be completely onboard.

As we set out on this path, we recognized from the beginning that the client journey had to be at the center of everything, which is why we began with our own client service charter that embodies our principles and sets out our service standards.

FBC Manby Bowdler LLP (FBCMB) has come an extremely long way, having put in a lot of work on all these fronts. The great news is that, having done so, we are now in the position of knowing that 97 percent of our clients are satisfied or very satisfied with what we do for them.

When we set out to achieve this, we knew that the process couldn't just be about meeting the demands of industry quality standards – though they certainly had a role. Instead, it had to be about standing out from everyone else by exceeding those standards at every turn.

We face a greater challenge than other, more client-focused, sectors, as consumers and our potential clients often have a poor view of the service they receive from our industry. The services we offer and the ways we deliver them can seem opaque and frustrating to those who are waiting to see the results of our efforts.

That makes communication one of the most important elements of providing legal and associated services. Careful and well managed communication cannot be a luxury add-on employed by an enlightened few – it should be at the heart of the organization.

We also recognized that we could not simply follow a path we presumed was correct. What we thought to be stellar service might not be how our clients would define it. We had to hear back from them, in as much detail as possible, and in as many numbers as possible.

Only this way could we properly define (and then refine) what it was to be outstanding in their eyes.

Defining "stellar"

Many discussions ensued internally about what this kind of outstanding service would look like. Definitions of what was acceptable, for instance in response times, could vary tremendously across departments. The involvement of all staff was essential in narrowing down these parameters, as was the LawNet Mark of Excellence[1] (for more on which see chapter ten).

We are members of LawNet, the collaborative network for independent law firms, and this charter mark was designed in response to the demands of member firms of the network and exists as an add-on to the existing LawNet ISO 9001 quality standard, which is obligatory for all members. Importantly, it brought to us a measurement-focused customer charter at its heart, with requirements for regular client service audits, both telephone and walk-in, alongside independently benchmarked online satisfaction questionnaires for clients.

Measuring and analyzing all of these client interactions is, of course, crucial. No less critical, however, is to drill down through the results, looking for every wrinkle to address and every opportunity to capitalize upon.

There can be surprises in what you discover when you are immersed in this process. For instance, many people really value the personalization, of contact in every part of the client journey, right through to the "thank you and farewell" stage of the current interaction. It would be easy to dismiss this part, because everyone has already got what was expected from the relationship and is ready to move on, but signing off properly really does carry weight and brings a satisfying closure to the job.

We also identified how important it is to examine all feedback as soon as you receive it, particularly when it is featured online, as it is on ReviewSolicitors.[2] Our marketing team looks at the responses we receive on a daily basis and takes any topics for discussion to team leaders to ensure they are quickly addressed. This has helped us keep our ReviewSolicitors rating at 4.8/5 after more than 1,200 reviews, as well as maintaining the firm's own client satisfaction scores.

A timely response to a criticism (however constructive) can be the crucial factor in making it a satisfactory response. It demonstrates a seriousness of purpose in gathering the feedback in the first place and it means that the issues at hand are more likely to be fresh in everyone's mind.

Where the person feeding back has taken the trouble to leave contact details in a survey or online, along with permission to follow-up with them, we make sure we call to thank them for taking the time and reassure them how much we value the feedback.

It's about leaving no stone unturned on this journey. For every survey completed we also make a donation to our corporate charities and ensure clients know that this will happen, giving them an extra incentive to invest their own time and to demonstrate that we intend to live by our CSR credentials.

All feedback we receive – both positive and constructive – is shared with the relevant lawyer and their team leader to help us to develop our service, highlighting the strengths of our service and potential areas for development.

We use comments from the surveys on our social media channels too using the hashtag #FeedbackFriday. This not only shows our customers what they can expect from us, it also gives the team a boost to see the great comments they have earned proudly shared with our followers.

An informed client feels involved – they have fewer questions requiring a telephone or email enquiry, they are likely to be more satisfied throughout, and at the end of the process. All those things being the case, they are much more likely to be a repeat client, to be open to suggested additional services that will clearly be of benefit to them and to be willing to give that all-important recommendation to others.

Central as they are to the entire process, the client can't be the sole object of the road to service excellence; it can only happen when every person in the firm understands, accepts, and is equipped to deliver the very best experience.

Bringing everyone on board

The FBCMB Stellar Service journey begins on induction when a new starter joins the firm. This is then followed with continuing discussion of "stellar" in department meetings and in one-to-one appraisals.

It's only right that when someone is seen to go above and beyond in their efforts to meet our vision of quality that they should be recognized for it. This happens in the form of choosing "Stellar Stars" throughout the year, based on both client and colleague feedback.

To reinforce the initial learning, "Stellar Service September" takes place annually, comprised of a week of training and activities focused on the ongoing importance of the customer service agenda.

Our process has needed to adjust and evolve a little over the past 18 months as we worked around the challenges of the pandemic and remote working, but the core learnings and ethos have remained the same throughout. Our clients need us to deliver, now more than ever.

With these, and many other, measures implemented, we are now a long way down the road of genuinely becoming a customer-service centered business – even with the bump in the road that was COVID-19. At this point there might be a danger of resting on our laurels or thinking that maintaining our current position will be enough. Of course, it's not.

The mindset must be that we have merely built the foundations of Stellar Service. The next few years must be about notching it up a further level. An important part of this must be in striving to provide a more holistic service. We have to change our mindset as lawyers yet again. We can't be like the doctor who sees the disease but not the patient; we must listen to each client and understand their problems, motivations, and objectives in order to identify the legal solutions that precisely meet their needs and expectations.

Continuing to improve is not just about our attitude and behavior. We also must look for how we can enhance the tools we use to deliver our service. Remote working, for example, may be part of firm life for some time to come and we need to ensure we are properly prepared to maintain and enhance the client experience we offer when we are unable to meet in person.

Sharpening the tools of our trade

Following careful evaluation, we are now integrating third-party services that will keep us at the cutting edge of how legal services can and should be delivered. Having already identified the crucial nature of communication in delivering satisfaction, this was an obvious area to focus on.

In 2021, we introduced the Perfect Portal[3] suite of tools at the firm to help us elevate our communications for smart phone and online users to further improve the experience for clients, while also making our operations more efficient. We rolled out the Perfect Portal app, currently available for residential property clients, for example, as a way to proactively communicate in processes with a higher rate of interaction, such as conveyancing. The app is free to the client and has been designed to give live case information, allowing clients to keep track of progress and see each step in the legal process. The app information can also be accessed via a web portal.

As much as the Perfect Portal app is a practical way of communicating using smart devices, it brings a feeling of being connected and involved in the case. When a task has been updated, clients receive a push notification, so there's no need to make a call or send an email to check on progress. This, of course, not only provides greater customer satisfaction, it can also have the very useful effect of cutting down time-consuming enquiries. Who doesn't welcome greater efficiency?

We've also introduced Perfect Portal's web intake forms for new residential enquiries as well as wills, LPAs and probate. It's just another way to make our communications with clients – and potential clients – more streamlined.

Another technical innovation was the introduction of DocuSign.[4] Rather than sending out agents to sign up personal injury clients, as is usual, we started asking customers if they would mind signing electronically, saving them around £50 to £100 each. The feedback was positive enough that we felt confident to begin a pilot with DocuSign. That pilot was a success, with many clients feeding back how easy to use the system was. We went ahead and launched it fully across the business in the middle of last year. It saved our clients a total of £17,000 and, as the cost per case is now so negligible, the firm itself pays the charge.

Another technology we've adopted is Settify[5] for our family department. This allows us to provide prospective clients with customized, helpful information about our services and it also gathers a comprehensive brief for us so we that we can tailor our response to the client from the very first call. First impressions count.

As a long-established profession with an obvious and understandable need to be cautious and thorough, it can be easier to eschew technological development in our field and rely on tried and tested methods. But technology is constantly evolving, so we need to be flexible and open to new ideas as they come to market. We've recently installed Introhive[6] to enhance our CRM to help us deliver a high-touch customer experience, and we are trialing HighQ[7] for our corporate team. HighQ is a collaborative site that can be used by both clients and our team, and it's really useful for complex projects where everything can be in one place. HighQ may be rolled out to other teams in the future should it continue to impress.

It's true that you have to move with care, attention to detail, and base decisions on solid evidence before bringing innovation to the delivery of our services. What is also true is that embracing new tools will be a crucial element of delivering ever greater client satisfaction. It can make every day processes easier, more efficient, and less costly.

Critically, the ability to improve communication is in everyone's interest. If it's done properly, clients will thank – and praise – you for it. You will reduce miscommunication and time spent answering enquiries.

What technology won't do is provide an instant fix for customer service deficiencies. New tools and services have a role to play, but they supplement the hard work and persistence involved in identifying what great customer service is, how to deliver it consistently, and how to bring everyone along with you in this continual journey to stand out from the crowd for all the right reasons.

How you do that in a world of ever-greater competition to provide services is now as important as how you deliver your legal expertise.

References

1. www.lawnet.co.uk/membership-benefits/practice-support/excellence-mark-client-care/
2. www.reviewsolicitors.co.uk/west-midlands/wolverhampton/fbc-manby-bowdler-llp
3. www.perfectportal.co.uk
4. www.docusign.co.uk
5. www.settify.co.uk
6. www.introhive.com
7. https://legal.thomsonreuters.com/en/products/highq/law-firms

Chapter 7:
Optimizing client service in the post-COVID legal market

By Douglas McPherson, director, Size 10½ Boots Ltd

Client service has never been so important. With so much else to worry about at the moment, this may sound like a strange thing to say. However, after such a traumatic year it is essential that your clients know their legal advisers absolutely have their best interests at heart, that they're on their side, that they are available to provide all of the assistance they need – either personally or professionally – to help them through the recovery and back into a more stable world.

When it comes to providing the optimal levels of client service, phrases like "All I need to do is stay available for my clients when they need me" and "Doing good work is all my clients want from me" simply will not cut it. Service is the element of working with you that your clients can see and feel, which means it is the element you must get right.

Your clients may not understand the technical intricacies of the work you do for them or how you found that all-important workaround to resolve the difficult situation they found themselves in. They will, however, know how easy it was to get hold of you, how you made them feel when they talked to you, how easy it was to access and implement their advice, and whether you offered/delivered more than they expected.

Service is not just a woolly, touchy-feely add on to your legal services. Service is what keeps your clients happy, it's what makes them feel valued, and it's what will ensure they stay your clients.

At this point I'd usually expect some push back. I'm told that if a client is a client, they will stay a client unless something particularly awful happens. That may have been true once, but it is certainly not the case now.

If we look at the key factors the pandemic has brought to the fore:

- Everyone is more cost-conscious than ever after a difficult year;
- Everyone is unsettled having faced issues we have never had to face before;

- Everyone has learned geography/proximity is no longer important in our working life, having adapted to working remotely for over a year; and
- Everyone has become even more reliant on sourcing suppliers (and, at the base level, lawyers are a supplier) online.

It is also becoming increasingly evident we are heading into a more volatile and unpredictable trading market. Admittedly, this is nothing new. The threat of boutique firms, alternative business structures, online delivery, and more rigorous formal procurement have been around for years. However, like the paperless office and more sustainable practices, we never quite got round to addressing these threats, largely because they have never had the impact we feared.

That is until now.

After such a seismic shift in working and purchasing practices, these threats are about to amplify regardless of the size, location, or specialisms of your firm.

Clients will shop around to find the best product at the best price and with the best service. With so much purchasing promiscuity in prospect, I am not exaggerating when I say that if you are not providing the optimal level of service, you could very well be placing the relationships upon which your practice and your firm are based in jeopardy.

But there is most definitely a huge up-side to investing in optimizing your client service.

If you provide the highest possible level of service and the best possible client experience, you will not only safeguard your retention rates but also continually open new conversations. Over time, if managed properly, these conversations will lead to more cross-selling opportunities.

Maintaining a closer proximity to clients who are more disposed towards you will also generate completely new opportunities, new introductions, and new insight into the groups, events, topics, and channels you could be using to market more effectively and win more new work.

And of course, the happier your clients are, the more likely they will be to refer you to their personal and professional networks, to their colleagues, families, and friends.

You don't need me to tell you that referrals are the best source of new opportunities. If you have been recommended by someone the enquirer trusts, the prospects will be easier and quicker to convert. This will immediately impact positively on both your pipeline and profitability.

It is also a source of new opportunities that costs you absolutely nothing other than providing the best possible client service.

How do you provide the best possible client service?

While this question can often cause huge consternation within a law firm, the answer actually lies very close to home.

If you are looking to optimize your client service offering, the best place to start is by asking yourself (and your partners and senior management team) what you consider to be the best client service. Is there a shop, hotel, or website that has really impressed you? Does your auditor, insurer, or bank do things that you think are above and beyond what you'd expect? Once you have a shortlist of businesses you enjoy engaging with you can work backwards and start to highlight what it is that they do that has impressed you.

Although everyone's answers will be different, I'd suggest the following all play a part in delivering the best possible client service.

Responsiveness

What we all want is to feel like we are being listened to. When we ask a question or ask for help, we want a response. This could be by phone, by email (even automated email), or in person but it needs to happen, and it needs to happen instantly.

Your response also needs to be designed to manage expectations. If the matter can't be dealt with there and then, you need to let the person know when they should expect a reply and how that reply will be sent.

When clients and prospective clients contact your firm, do they get an immediate response? How do you let them know their question has been received?

Action

Following on from the response, people want to see their enquiry is being dealt with. There is nothing more irritating than feeling you have been left in a holding pen or worse, fallen into a big black hole. Remember that people go to a lawyer for very specific reasons and however minor these reasons may be, they will be the most important thing in your client's life at that moment. This means they must see action.

If you have designed your response to include next steps and timelines, make sure these are met. Not meeting the deadlines you have set yourself will sow seeds of doubt in the minds of your clients. Over time that doubt could very well lead to them seeking alternative advisers.

Better still, pad out your timelines and beat them. The psychological effect of under-promising and overdelivering is always positive.

If the matter at hand is going to take a while to resolve, provide regular updates so your clients know you are making progress and are completely up to date with exactly where you are and what to expect next.

How do you currently update your clients? How could you improve the way you communicate your progress and let your clients know where they are and what to expect next?

Ease of use

Regardless of which sector you operate in, ease of use will always be a major factor in maximizing your repeat purchase rate. As this new digitally driven landscape is increasing the number and availability of different options, while the importance of location continues to diminish, ease of use will only become more important to your clients.

In terms of making a law firm easy to use you should consider the following factors:

- How easy are you to find online? Are you coming out near the top of the organic searches most relevant to your practice areas and sector specialisms?
- Once you reach your website, how easy is it to find the information you want and the fee earner you need to speak to?
- Once you've identified who you need to speak to, how easy is it to get in touch with them? Do you have clear (and working) response mechanisms?
- If you are already a client, how easy is it to reach your lawyer? Are they easily accessible and (again) responsive?
- When you receive communications from the firm, are they easy to understand and implement?
- When clients want additional non-legal advice, how easy do you make it for them to get an introduction to the right people in your professional network?
- Is it easy to get to see you when your clients need to see you? Do you make yourself available for on and offsite and virtual meetings?
- When your clients come to your office do you make it easy to park and find the right meeting room?

- Do you do more to make your clients lives easier when they are onsite? Can they charge their phones and other devices? Do you provide telephone answering, printing, or copying facilities? Do you have reading glasses they can borrow if needs be?
- Is it easy to bump into you at the relevant local and industry events?

I have heard in the past that these are "little things" compared with the provision of high-quality legal advice. This is hugely short sighted. Not only do the little things have the biggest impact, but these are the things your clients experience first-hand. They are also the things that will make them keep coming back and refer you to their family and friends.

Is your firm easy to use? Have you asked your clients what would make the firm easier to use?

Product knowledge

There is nothing more irritating than contacting a business and being met (physically or virtually) by someone who doesn't know what they're talking about. They might try and pull the wool over your eyes by just talking and talking (and, more than likely, talking nonsense) or they might try and park you by saying they need to refer you to someone else. Whichever path they take, your firm's credibility will be severely damaged.

You need to make sure that your front of house staff knows:

- What every practice area does;
- Who in the firm they should refer specific enquiries to;
- How to book meetings with these lawyers;
- Who is in/available at that time and who isn't; and
- How to acknowledge and confirm what will happen next.

This will involve constant training, which will require time and budget, but as the alternative is leaving clients nervous, underwhelmed, and ultimately looking for a new lawyer, it will be time and budget well spent.

You can also complete the external perception of your product knowledge by supplementing the way your team handles enquiries by adding chatbots to your website. This is covered in the next chapter but by using very basic artificial intelligence you can program your bots to take clients and prosects through a logical stream of questioning that will show them you understand what they want and know how to get them to the lawyer they need to speak to.

If someone were to contact your firm today, would they be greeted with the level of product knowledge they'd expect? Or do you need to make improvements in the levels of understanding your front of house staff offer?

Clear direction

When we interview our clients' clients during client listening programs, one of the questions we ask is what the client's critical success factors are. What do they have to receive in return for the fees they are paying their advisers?

One of the most common factors clients put forward – albeit in different words – is clear direction. They tell me they don't want the old-fashioned low/medium/high risk options. They don't want to hear what they can't do. They don't want wishy-washy maybes cloaked in impenetrable legalese. They want clear advice. They want to hear what their lawyer would do if they were in their position and needed to achieve their desired outcome.

While clear direction may not be something you'd immediately assimilate with optimal client service, it is one thing that clients definitely want and therefore has to be a part of your service offering.

Clear next steps

Uncertainty unsettles clients. You need to provide your clients with updates on your progress and explain what will happen next, confirm by when this will happen, and then make sure you hit the deadlines you've set. Although you understand all the legal processes and probable outcomes involved in the work you are doing for a client, you must assume the client doesn't and take the lead in terms of managing their expectations and explaining what you are doing and why.

Added value

In my experience, added value is something all clients crave but many firms still concentrate on the "added" rather than the "value".

Newsletters, seminars, and blogs are all fine (and effective marketing vehicles) but they are very much add-ons rather than valuable. Real value is being there as and when your clients need you, being willing to answer quick questions as they arise, and providing not just the black letter law answer but "in your shoes" advice – clear and focused advice that provides the clear direction we looked at earlier.

It's about opening up your personal and professional networks to your clients, making it easier for them to establish the connections they need to make to further their personal and business objectives. It's about taking time out to talk to them about where they are, where they're going, and providing the support they need to get there. It's about pulling your clients' lives or businesses apart so you can see how best to help them. For example, if you are an employment lawyer, can you provide training for your clients' management teams? Can you send one of your junior colleagues onsite for two days a month on secondment to support their HR function? Can you provide content for their staff intranet?

All of this boils down to one thing – conversations. And I don't mean conversations about open matters or recently closed files. I mean just chatting things through, taking an interest, really getting to know your clients. Sometimes I am challenged when I suggest just meeting up for a catch up. "But my clients are busy people, they don't have time to talk to me!" I am told. I have to say that when I finally do persuade them to set up that coffee/lunch/visit, the client is always appreciative and tells their lawyer so.

Better still, almost all these conversations uncover new opportunities, which means the other common objection I hear ("I can't take time away from the office, I need to deliver my billable hours") is quashed. You may have lost a couple of billable hours, but you will more than recoup these with the new work you win.

What do you have in place to find out what your clients value? And how are you using this insight to improve your client service?

Service but not "over service"

This may sound strange but over service can be as off putting as bad service. There is a marked difference between respect and obsequiousness. Clients want to be warmly welcomed and well looked after when they are in your company and in your offices, but they don't want bowing and scraping.

How do you put the improvements you want to make into practice?

In the previous section I asked a number of questions about the different areas that make up optimal client service. Before you can make any improvements, you need to know where you are so I would strongly suggest you form a working group to answer these questions and answer them honestly. This working group should include lawyers at both ends of their career (not just partners, as while they will have the closest client contact, they can be – shall we say – somewhat set in their ways) from each of your practice areas, front of house staff (they're on the front line, after all), and your marketing/business development manager/director.

I would also include clients. I appreciate this will make some within the firm nervous, but they are the ones whose opinions really matter. They are the ones paying the money to receive your services, which means their feedback is the most important.

This feedback can be garnered in three ways:

1. The client partner can arrange an informal catch up and use the opportunity to ask a few questions about they way they are looked after, what else they need, where improvements can be made, and any other business.
2. You can invest in an independent client listening program whereby an experienced interviewer talks to your clients. Many firms still send their senior partner or a partner from another department to conduct these interviews, but I would always recommend you engage an external interviewer. Although your partners will do a great job, they still have the firm's name on their business cards so the interviewee may hold back a little out of politeness. An external interviewer will receive a much more rounded picture and, as they are experienced in interviewing clients, be able to spot the areas to dig a little deeper and encourage even more candid feedback.
3. You can do both of the above and compare the results.

Once you have your answers you will be able to spot where you need to make improvements and you can begin to tackle the implementation. Although the steps will of course vary from firm to firm, the one thing every implementation has in common for success is dependent on consistency. Everyone needs to buy in and take-up needs to be universal.

One way to achieve this is to create what I've variously seen called a client charter, a client value proposition, or "*The [insert firm's name] Way*".

This sets out what you expect of your lawyers in terms of how they service their relationships and how they deliver their work. I would support the launch of your charter with training for all fee earners and separate sessions for your front of house staff. I would also make this training a feature of your induction program to make sure all your service objectives are ingrained in your lawyers from day one. You can also make your intentions public by posting a version of your charter on your website and support that with testimonials from your clients confirming this really is the way you work and how your way of working has benefited them.

You can also use your service proposition and your clients' comments in your marketing material, pitches, and tenders. The majority of brochures and tenders I'm asked to review still concentrate on the firm, how many offices and lawyers it has, and when it was founded before repeating a bit of anodyne content from its "About Us" page. Unfortunately, no one cares about this stuff. People want to know what it's like to work with you and what else they'll get if they choose you. When it comes to marketing or the formal procurement process, you need to stand out as the best choice. What better way of doing that than to show those judging your bid how well looked after they will be? This will appeal to their sense of self in a way that copying in chunks of your website never will.

Finally, what gets measured gets done so I would also suggest putting checks in place to make sure the promised delivery and response times are being met, that emails are being responded to, that the right levels of personal access are being provided and that there are client development plans in place (and in progress) for the relevant clients.

Again, an annual client listening exercise can also play a valuable role in achieving consistency and monitoring your progress, not to mention unearthing more testimonials and quotes that you can use online and in pitches and your marketing material.

How do you ensure you are delivering the optimal levels of client service while working in a hybrid environment?

Everything we've looked at in this chapter is based on working the traditional way, in teams and in offices. However, it is very probable things will never be the same again in terms of the way we work. The most likely scenario is we will end up working in what is being referred to as a "hybrid" environment – a few days in the office and a few days at home each week.

This does not need to impact on the levels of service you offer your clients.

All the individual elements that go into delivering optimal client service – responsiveness, action, ease of use, product knowledge, clear direction, clear next steps, added value – can all be delivered from wherever you are working thanks to the technology we have all become very familiar with during 2020 and 2021.

The new video conferencing platforms are not the only tool at our disposal when it comes to maintaining contact with our clients. There is another much more old-fashioned tool that has proved crucial to keeping our own business going during the two lengthy lockdowns in the UK – the phone. While people have been working at home, we've found clients are much more receptive to a phone call, if only to speak to someone outside their usual immediate circle. This is as true with senior members of the partnership as it is with the more junior lawyers we are providing business development coaching for.

Moreover, people are willing to talk for longer on the phone. If you consider that the purchasing decision clients make to use any professional adviser is influenced in even amounts by your technical skills and your personal fit, the small talk around these calls can provide some hugely valuable insight. You find out what clients like to do, drink, or eat. Once you know which sports, cuisine, films, or music each is partial to, where they want to go on holiday once restrictions ease or what their children are doing, you will always have something to talk about and always have a reason to drop them a line should you see something relevant online or in the newspaper.

This is real client care. Taking an interest in your clients, personalizing your approach, and underlining the fact you are there for them as a person, not as a file number or your next invoice.

Similarly, client listening is an exercise that can also work on a virtual basis. I'll be honest, it does still work best face-to-face as meeting in person allows you to establish a better rapport, assess the person's body language, and make sure they are not distracted by deliveries, emails, and all the other things that disrupt a day's working from home, but video interviews do work for the clients you either can't travel to see or are not comfortable yet meeting in person.

The only problem is while we are working remotely and on our own, client development – in fact, all types of marketing and business development – can quickly fall victim to the rule of out of sight, out of mind.

As there's no one asking you about client development, it is easy to park it in favor of doing your legal work. This is not an option. Just because you're working somewhere else doesn't mean your responsibility to providing the highest level of service for your clients has changed. In all likelihood they will be working somewhere different too, so you just have to find a way to stay in touch that suits you both.

This alone will need a conversation – which is another opportunity to chat and ask questions about what else you could be doing for your client and glean even more insight into what you need to do to optimize your client service.

Chapter 8:
Are automated assistants ready to optimize the next chapter of online client care?

By James Matthews, UK&I country manager, CM.com

Law firms have a fine line to tread. On the one hand, one of the things clients repeatedly complain about is their inability to get hold of who they need when they need to. On the other, as people, we want to get what we need as quickly as possible but more and more we want to do this without actually having to speak to anyone! We will search online. We will email. We will fill in and submit forms. In fact, we will do pretty much anything as long as we don't actually have to ring an unfamiliar number and spend time explaining our situation in detail to someone we don't know. Part of the reason for this is the way calls tend to be handled. All too often the person we speak to doesn't really understand what we're asking for. They may be inexperienced, temporary, or poorly trained. Whatever the reason is, we know there is a chance we will be placed in an interminable holding pattern as the call is bounced around departments until the right person is found. Or worse still, we're told someone will ring back (without being told who or when this will be). Admittedly, training can play a huge part here but there is still a propensity for error and that error could end up costing you a client and, further down the line, a potential ambassador for the firm.

However, imagine if all the enquiries you received through your website and the search engines were handled immediately, flawlessly, and efficiently, irrespective of where they came from, what they want, and what time of day (or night) they arise? This may sound like an implausible pipe-dream but there is a solution. It is a solution more and more law firms are considering as they look to optimize the level of care they afford clients and prospective clients at the first point of contact.

Is LegalTech the springboard to a higher level of client service?

LegalTech is simply the umbrella term for the various technologies that have been designed specifically to help change the way legal services are facilitated and delivered. Over the last few years, the concept of LegalTech has really taken hold but up to this point it has largely been equated with workflow, delivery, and improving internal efficiencies. Although it is still very much in its infancy, those firms that have already started to implement the available technologies have seen dramatic improvements in the way they work, including:

- Increased productivity;
- Improved resource management;
- Reduced operating costs;
- An increase in accuracy and a reduction in human error;
- Enhanced employee engagement; and
- Increased profitability.

Increased profitability (particularly during what is arguably the most competitive and challenging trading environment law firms have ever had to contend with) is of course the most compelling argument for LegalTech for partners of law firms of every size. However, profitability can be increased further still if you look beyond simply reducing staff costs and increasing operational efficiencies. If you were to reinforce the impact of both these factors with happier clients, with more clients, and with clients who are more likely to make a more significant contribution to both your revenues and your pipeline of new work, you would be enjoying an increase in revenue in addition to a reduction in costs and improved operational efficiencies. Automating many of the ways you communicate with clients will improve the level of client care you provide. At the highest level, the fact that your fee earners and support staff can leave some of the administrative tasks to your tech means more of their time can be spent on your clients. This could mean more time with clients at the senior end, finding ways to add more value to the relationship (even if that's via the partner), in more subtle ways at the more junior end, or just making things happen more quickly and easily if you are in a support role. However, from a more practical perspective, the client care objectives you may want to source solutions to tackle could include the following.

1. Improved communication

Consistent updates and managing expectations are two of the issues clients bring up most often when they're asked about the level of service provided by their law firm. When a firm gets it right, they are praised but it is more often the case that the client has to ask for updates. This rankles with them. Basic AI can automate some of these updates by monitoring the firm's case management systems to pick up on completed milestones and sending a personalized message out to clients to confirm this part of the work has been done and letting them know what will come next and by when.

2. Improved onboarding

Clumsy onboarding is another issue that irritates clients. Using technology to make this easier for clients will have a hugely positive impact on the earliest stages of your relationship. Moreover, it will also have a positive impact internally. The easier it is to onboard a client, the less time and expense will be involved. Again, this will improve profitability.

3. Increased speed of response

As most LegalTech is designed to improve productivity, its implementation will help you improve your client experience. The quicker you can return work and the less human error/unanswered questions it throws up, the happier your clients will be, and a happy client is much more likely to come back to you for either more of the same or to ask for advice from different practice areas. Similarly, they will be much more likely to refer their personal and professional networks, and these referrals will generate even more new clients.

4. Increased data security

Since the GDPR came into force in May 2018 and reports of cyber-attacks involving law firms continue to hit the headlines, it has never been as vital to ensure your client and financial data is totally secure. This factor has taken on even greater significance whilst people have been working from home, as more data is being shared every day remotely and across multiple locations. A breach could cause irreparable reputational damage to your firm, damage that could impact on both your existing client relationships and on your ability to bring in new clients.

Where to start?

If you are new to LegalTech or only just beginning to start to take advantage of the benefits it offers, these may all seem like lofty aspirations and, by extension, expensive projects to embark upon. The good news though is there are a raft of more accessible, more implementable, and more affordable technologies open to you that make an immediate impact on your client care offering. Arguably the most accessible, implementable, and affordable solution is one that can tackle one of the other complaints those looking to purchase legal services put forward most often – how difficult it is to navigate around a website and find the right person to provide the required advice. It is a gripe that is amplified when advice is being sought, as is more and more often the case, outside of office hours. The solution is the virtual assistant.

Virtual assistants – a simple starting point

Every law firm has invested heavily in their website. They know how essential it is to have an online presence that represents who they are and what they do in the sharpest and most visually striking way. However, legal websites are currently entering what we feel is their third generation. The first generation of websites were nothing more than online brochures. They had to look good (again, it is an online representation of the firm, so it needs to impress) but other than offering a smart navigable design, they didn't actually do anything. The second generation of websites started to do more. An increased number of calls-to-action invited visitors to interact with the firm, to ask for more information, to speak to a fee earner or to sign up for regular updates on a specific topic or follow the firm on social media. Meanwhile, blogs, articles and, more recently, infographics and video encouraged visitors to keep coming back to a website whilst improving the firm's search engine rankings to encourage more first-time visitors to the site. An increasing number of firms have also added "live chat" features so that visitors can ask questions instead of having to look around the site themselves.

The third generation will take this initial level of interaction even further. Websites are set to become even more intuitive. This in turn will maximize the user experience for your prospective clients and, just as importantly, maximize the results (most notably in terms of convertible new enquiries) your site generates. While live chat is a great start, using this functionality will depend completely on how busy people are, how much time they have, and on an assumption that visitors actually know what they want when they get to the website. The question of time (or, in fact, timing) is even more pertinent in the post-COVID era. As people's schedules are more fluid and the demands on their time are more challenging, sourcing legal advice is something that is likely to be pushed down the to do list during the day. It is something that will probably be done in the evening or at the weekend which, unless the response has been outsourced, is when law firms won't have anyone on call to man the live chat.

This presents firms with a dilemma. Do you outsource the management of your live chat? There's obviously an additional cost involved here (not to mention a training cost as you can't afford to have your function manned by people who don't know your services and staff inside out). You'll need to work out whether that cost outweighs the potential level/value of enquiries the function will generate. Or do you man your live chat with existing resources? This would be an addition to their existing responsibilities, which could mean their coverage is questionable during their busiest times. Or do you simply carry on relying on visitors filling in your "contact us" form or sending you an email so you can initiate a manual response within 24 hours?

This is the option that is perhaps most appealing. It allows you to provide a response but in your own time and around the other demands of your day. However, it is a manual process open to human error. It can get lost or forgotten and even if you only misplace one in 20 enquiries, that one could be the lucrative long-term client your website has been designed to capture. Buyer behavior also needs to be considered. If someone is searching for something online, they will be looking at more than one potential supplier. If your response isn't instant, they will move onto another firm's website, then another, then another. By the time you have replied, they could already be deep in conversation with one of your competitors, which means the opportunity has been lost. Similarly, in today's world you will only get one bite at the cherry. If an enquiry is lodged but the response isn't fast, your prospective client will be irritated with the service they've received so will never come back to you. More damagingly, they could even mention their experience to their network, which could dissuade others from using your firm. With the third generation of websites, the key will be to use technology to make things as simple but immediate as possible and use the content and the knowledge you have to make your website work for you and provide your prospective clients with a superior experience and an optimal level of client service from their first interaction with your firm.

Virtual assistants could be a simple first step to making this aim a reality. As they are an "off the shelf" solution, they can be added to any law firm's website and programmed to give your visitors the care, attention, and answers they want, irrespective of when they visit and what they want to find out. They will effortlessly guide your visitors to the answers and information they want and introduce them to the right fee earner. They can even make a virtual introduction to set the wheels in motion there and then. From a more practical – not to mention financial – perspective, they will capture more prospective clients and direct them – faster and more efficiently – towards conversion.

How could a virtual assistant improve your client care?

The first question to ask yourself is what you want your website to achieve. Do you want it to become a booking clerk or give visitors initial advice? If it is the former, you need to capitalize on the content you already have – your blogs, articles, FAQs, white papers, downloads, and video content. By programming a series of questions, you can take your client from an automated but personalized greeting to specific pieces of content by linking the key words in their responses to the key words behind your content. Even if the visitor isn't 100 percent sure of exactly what they need, your understanding of the subject matter and the likely route a client will take to determine what they want will allow you to create viable chains of questions that will direct them to exactly what they want. Once they have reached the desired page you can then introduce them to the author and offer an initial call or virtual or physical meeting (this process can be made even more efficient by linking your assistant to your shared calendars, your meeting room system, and/or Teams or Zoom accounts).

From a user perspective this journey is extremely easy. There is no annoying form to fill in as you'll be able to capture their details as you progress. For example, asking what their name is at the start will allow you to initiate a more personalized conversation. Then, once you have their name, you can capture their email address by asking if they'd like regular updates on certain topics once you've identified the topics they're interested in. Using your virtual assistant to provide initial pieces of advice would follow a similar process, albeit with slightly more advanced questioning. I should also say that when I am talking about providing advice, this is not legal advice per se. That would open a minefield of potential indemnity issues. What I mean is suggesting viable next steps. For example, if the visitor is looking to start the process of planning for their and their families' future, then the first step would be for them and their partner to have a new will drafted. Your assistant can tell them this should be done in consultation with an experienced private client lawyer as there will undoubtedly be major tax considerations to tackle as these will directly impact on their beneficiaries' inheritances. You could even offer a download covering the potential tax implications there and then to tie the visitor in further. While this is a very simplistic example, the theory can be applied to almost any scenario.

If the visitor was looking to set up a new company, then the answer they are led to could be a "new company checklist" setting out all the paperwork they'll need – their articles of incorporation, a shareholders' agreement, trademark protection for their brand, a standard employment contract, a customer contract, terms and conditions for their website, etc. This could also be linked to an automated meeting request to put them in touch with a new business specialist in your commercial team to tie the visitor in and keep your conversation moving forward.

How can virtual assistants be used to improve the way you market and the results your marketing achieves?

The immediate objective of adding a virtual assistant to your website is of course to generate new introductions, new conversations, and book new meetings. However, the "live" answers you receive will also offer a hugely valuable insight into what your clients want – insight you can use to improve your marketing. The first step in this process is to use the responses and chains of responses to improve the way your assistant operates. The more relevant questions your virtual assistant can ask, the more useful the answers will be to the visitor, and the more useful the answers are, the more likely your assistant will be to maintain their interest all the way to the final "book a meeting" option. More importantly, the more useful your visitors find your website, the more likely they will be to revisit and reuse your site to find out what they need to know. The more times someone visits your site, the more likely they will be to purchase your services. This process is of course a moving feast. To get the most out of your assistant – and to ensure your visitors get the most out of your assistant and the content behind it – you will need to continually assess:

- The questions being asked;
- The information sets relating to these questions;
- The efficacy with which your questions lead visitors to these information sets; and
- The level of enquiries that last the distance and convert into enquiries and/meetings.

This assessment will also highlight the holes. Where are lines of questioning breaking down? At what stage are people leaving the conversation? Once you can see the patterns you can highlight if more questions are needed to better direct people to the conclusion they want or, indeed, if there are too many questions to answer. The next stage is to use the types of questions to identify the service areas people are asking about most frequently. These are the areas your content marketing should be focusing on.

1. Future blogs

These blogs will be added to your site to help your virtual assistant direct visitors to an even broader range of relevant content and make it more likely they will respond and take the ultimate step – contacting you for more information. However, having more content on the areas your clients are asking about most frequently will also feed the search engines and improve your organic search rankings to create even more new opportunities.

2. Video and audio content

Video (infographics and talking heads) and audio (predominantly podcasts) are very popular with clients at the moment. As with your blogs, the insight your virtual assistant will provide will make sure you are talking about (or animating) the right parts of the right topics so you maximize your audience.

3. External publishing opportunities

Being published in the trade or local publications your clients and targets read is a productive and cost-effective way to get in front of a new audience. As you will constantly be on top of what your clients want to know about, you will be able to offer editors articles that tackle what their readers want to know. As you know exactly what questions are being asked, your articles will really be able to provide all the specific detail their readers need.

4. Seminars/workshops

Whether restrictions allow you to deliver your educational events in person or whether you will need to continue to deliver them virtually, the insight you'll receive from your virtual assistant will ensure the content of your seminars and sessions is totally on point, which will positively impact on attendee numbers and on the scores you receive for value and relevance on the post-event feedback form (which in turn will increase the percentage of re-bookings for future events). Better still, you should also be able to use the questions asked/points raised/key discussion points to improve your virtual assistant's script. The other aspect of this insight that will make a huge difference to both your conversion rates and the level of client care you are providing is training. The rate at which the enquiries your virtual assistant are converted by the member of your team that handles them will highlight what is working and what isn't. Both sets of data have to be observed to ensure you continue to develop. Be prepared to share success stories so people know what is working and what clients are responding to. Getting the people on the front line together to talk about the words and actions they feel have led directly to new client wins will not only give people a few tips and tricks they can employ themselves, it will also show you what prospective clients are responding to. All these words/phrases/offers can be incorporated into your virtual assistant's script moving forward.

Identifying what isn't working will highlight where additional training may be required. This could be sales training to help them move a conversation forward, pricing training so that more attractive (but still profitable) quotes can be made there and then on a call, or basic client care techniques. The good news is whichever areas require training, the effects will have a much more extensive impact on the firm's commercial performance. They will teach techniques that your fee earners can use to win new work and provide an even higher standard of client care throughout their careers and throughout each of your clients' association with the firm.

In summary, virtual assistants are not a replacement for staff or technology. The true power of using a virtual assistant lies in the additional benefits it brings – the primary benefit being better quality of service which, in turn, leads to more clients, referrals, and better retention. But virtual assistants are by no means a golden bullet for high quality service. They need to be regularly evaluated, assessed and iteratively improved as the business and/or portfolio of services and content grows. But, when managed correctly, virtual assistants can free up fee earners to focus on the parts of the job that matter, and deliver dedicated customer service around the clock.

Chapter 9: Innovation as a business development strategy

By Scott Rechtschaffen, chief knowledge officer at Littler Mendelson

Law firm marketing approaches have evolved

Consider the marketing phrases that law firms have used to differentiate themselves from their competition. Once, law firm collateral, websites, and advertising focused on "great lawyering" – essentially, saying their attorneys are smarter and more skilled than attorneys at other firms. Then, law firm marketing shifted to a focus on "partnering" and "collaborating" with clients – claiming their attorneys understood clients' business better than the attorneys at other firms.

But how exactly does a firm – say, a firm ranked as number 76 on the AmLaw 100 list – demonstrate through its website or advertising copy that its attorneys are smarter, or that they are better client partners than, say, the attorneys at a firm ranked as AmLaw number 39, 79, or 86? With bios showing where its attorneys went to law school? With lists or anonymized case studies? Can law firms seriously market their advantage over competitors with claims of greater intellectual prowess or saying they are more cost effective? Saying so does not necessarily make these firms a better value. Are these really the attributes that distinguish one law firm from another? Firms highlight their attorneys' knowledge of a client's business and its industry. It is impossible to be a great lawyer without that, but it's not a differentiator – it's table stakes.

Recently, many law firms have begun to focus their marketing and brand-building efforts on a tangible attribute to significantly differentiate themselves from the competition using the phrase "Innovation." But true "innovation" is more than a passing buzzword, or the marketing phrase of the moment. Innovation must be part of a dedicated strategic plan to improve the delivery of legal services and positively impact the law firm–client relationship to the benefit of both. Innovation strategies include developing robust knowledge management programs, providing clients with transparent legal information offerings, implementing legal process management and legal process improvement methodologies, and deploying genuinely cutting-edge technology (i.e. beyond iPhone and Android apps, sophisticated websites, and extranets).

Why innovation is relevant for today's corporate legal clients

Developing an innovation strategy is much more than a marketing device because innovation, used this way, addresses the most critical demands that corporate legal clients are now making of their outside counsel. Since the Great Recession of 2008 and its impact on the legal industry, clients have increasingly demanded a change in the way their law firms deliver services. For most firms, the days of routine annual rate increases and ill-defined – or "blank check" – budgets for legal matters are a distant memory from the golden days of the legal industry. Now, clients demand reduced costs, increased efficiency, greater transparency, and higher quality standards. In-house counsel have greater leverage than ever to change the way their outside counsel deliver legal services. Corporate clients also have more options to get the legal resources they need. What many attorneys and law firms do not realize is that they are no longer just competing with other law firms; they are competing with Google and the vast array of resources that the web offers.

Today, an innovation strategy has to be much more than the technology "innovations" that law firms have adopted over the past decades – email, smartphones, online legal research, extranets, and e-filing. These have been sustainable innovations enabling lawyers to communicate and collaborate with their clients more efficiently, but they did not fundamentally change how legal services were delivered and by whom. Newly emerging technologies – for example, predictive coding, document automation, and "expert advisor" systems, such as Littler's ComplianceHR suite of products, discussed below – are disruptive technologies. Over time, they will vastly reduce the need for, respectively, attorney-performed document review, attorneys drafting routine documents, and attorneys answering basic client questions.

Legal services have largely remained a one-attorney-to-one-user interaction model (or a many-attorney-to-one-client model). But the rest of the world leverages technology on a one-provider-to-hundreds-or-thousands-of-users model. It is unreasonable to believe that lawyers will remain a unique coterie of professionals delivering bespoke services, while the rest of the world – including every other major profession – has moved further into the online mainstream. As legal industry prognosticator Richard Susskind has noted: "It is simply inconceivable that information technology will radically alter all corners of our economy and society and yet somehow legal work will be exempt from any change."[1]

For innovation to become more than just a marketing phrase, for a law firm to truly establish its brand as an "innovative" law firm, it must develop and implement a strategy that truly transforms how legal services – legal information, litigation, advice and counseling, transactional work – are delivered. It is insufficient to simply "check the box" by launching one or two apps or adding more generic articles and news alerts to a firm's website. A true innovation strategy envisions dramatically and comprehensively changing the way firms interact with and serve their clients that helps clients make money, save money, look good, or sleep better. A successful innovation strategy cannot just change the game, it has to change it for the better.

Innovation at Littler

At Littler, we have spent the past three decades developing and implementing just such an innovation strategy. We began by offering clients a robust knowledge management program, with a content marketing strategy that delivered critical, valuable legal, business, and legislative insights in a way that other firms could seldom match. More recently, though, we have moved to develop technology tools, legal processes, and products that offer our clients alternatives to the traditional one-to-one client-attorney relationship and the billable hour model.

Through these efforts, Littler has become widely recognized as an innovative law firm – it has become a core component of our brand, if you will. Over the past few years, we have been consistently recognized by major publications, and both the firm and our individual attorneys have received awards for innovation. Increasingly, we are hearing clients reference our investment in innovative service solutions as a differentiator.

The beginnings of innovation at Littler – knowledge management

About 20 years ago, a number of major US law firms began adding knowledge management functions to their corporate infrastructure. Many hired chief knowledge officers or directors of knowledge management. Initially, the goal was to enhance access to the treasure trove of precedential work product that law firms seemingly generate in their sleep – model transactional documents, best practice forms and policies, pleadings and litigation documents, and advice memos. In those early days, knowledge management was designed to prevent lawyers from constantly reinventing the wheel by providing them with access to the best work product already created by experienced colleagues within their firms. This would, of course, increase efficiency and save clients time and money.

Naturally, many firms turned to technology solutions. Often, knowledge management became an adjunct to the IT department and the leading advocates for knowledge management were those law firm partners who had a real passion for and fascination with technology. Firms developed and deployed expertise databases, enterprise search systems, and elaborate subject-matter intranets. At Littler, our knowledge management program similarly focused initially on providing the firm's attorneys with ready access to the enormous amount of precedential work product created by the firm's subject matter experts. We developed internal databases and collections of substantive materials. We deployed an enterprise search tool that enabled attorneys to quickly find the work product they needed to work more efficiently and avoid recreating the wheel in serving their clients.

However, Littler realized that focusing knowledge management solely on improving internal attorney efficiency ignored the advantages that a robust knowledge management program could contribute to the firm's service to its clients, as well as the firm's brand and overall marketing efforts.

Knowledge management as the foundation of a comprehensive content marketing strategy

Recognizing the value and importance of truly leveraging firm-created content, Littler's knowledge management program began to focus extensively on creating and aggregating valuable substantive content in ways that informed clients of critical developments and demonstrated the firm's deep and broad subject matter expertise. This was a natural evolution of Littler's already heavy investment in content dissemination that demonstrated its substantive legal knowledge and analysis. Littler first published *The National Employer®* book before it had a single office outside of California – which naturally helped develop Littler's brand as a national law firm even before we were truly national in geographic scope. Similarly, Littler published its *Guide to International Employment and Labor Law* before it had a single office outside of the United States – again, helping to develop Littler's global brand before we had a presence in 25 countries, as we do today. In both instances, the smart development and distribution of content helped define Littler's brand, providing a natural base for our knowledge and expertise.

Initially, these knowledge management efforts included not only client conferences, client alerts, and newsletters, but also comprehensive compendiums with in-depth analysis of pertinent legal issues and developments. Some of these publications and content initiatives are:

- **The Employer Series publications:** Littler developed this print publication series over 30 years ago to be a comprehensive primer of employment and labor law. Initially, *The National Employer®* book was created as a loose-leaf notebook designed to be handed out at client conferences. Over time, Littler developed relationships with major legal content publishers to transform that thin notebook into an exhaustive 6,000-plus page encyclopedia covering federal law and the law of 50 states and the District of Columbia – published in both print and digitally. Recently, we completely overhauled our approach to these publications, converting them into the *Littler on* series, a collection of over 30 titles, each one focused on a specific area of employment law such as *Littler on Corporate Restructuring, Littler on Disability in the Workplace*, and *Littler on Religion in the Workplace.*[2]
- **Legal development alerts:** Littler typically publishes over 400 legal development alerts each year in various formats – as electronic newsletters, client alerts, and blog posts.[3] During the pandemic, Littler published over 950 client alert publications and offered clients a subscription to a daily COVID-19 newsflash. These are sent directly to clients, posted on the firm's website, posted to social media sites, and distributed through various channels such as Mondaq, Lexology, JD Supra, and others. At one point, Littler maintained 11 separate blogs covering topics as diverse as workplace privacy, global employment law developments, global immigration, electronic discovery, and wage-hour law. (Littler's blogs have since been incorporated into Littler's overall content platform and no longer exist as stand-alone blogs.)
- **White papers and Littler reports:** Every year, Littler publishes in-depth white papers and reports covering major developments and coming trends in employment and labor law. Littler's *Annual Report on EEOC Developments*[4] has been published annually for the past five years and provides a comprehensive examination of significant events and enforcement activities of the Equal Employment Opportunity Commission. Weekly, Littler publishes the *WPI Weekly Wrap-Up* and the *WPI Labor Day Report*[5] – both comprehensive reports by Littler's Workplace Policy Institute providing in-depth analysis of legislative and regulatory developments at the federal, state, and local levels. In 2021, Littler published its *Workforce Transformation Report*,[6] a comprehensive white paper prepared by 35 Littler attorneys examining the changes to the workplace and workforce brought on

by robotics and artificial intelligence, the move to remote work, and other changes accelerated by COVID-19.

- **Single-subject publications:** Littler has also worked with many of the major legal industry publishers on books dedicated to specific topics within the field of employment and labor law. Our attorneys have developed authoritative publications that enable us to say, truly, that "we wrote the book" on major subject areas of interest to our clients.

The CEO of one of the leading online legal research platforms observed that, with its prolific output, Littler must surely rank as one of the top ten leading producers of legal content in the US. He then asked how Littler was able to generate such a huge volume of content given that most attorneys are generally incentivized and compensated for generating client work, not writing books and white papers.

How do we do it?

There are really several answers to this question. First, with its long history of using content to market the firm's authoritative knowledge and expertise in the field of employment and labor law, it has become part of our culture that attorneys are expected to contribute to the firm's publishing efforts. Second, Littler has always stressed the importance of individual attorneys becoming "subject matters experts" in the many sub-domains that make up the field of employment and labor law. Attorneys who wish to develop business and new clients – and get referrals of business from within the firm – are encouraged to establish themselves in fields that are critical to our clients, such as privacy, employee benefits, executive compensation, and union-management relations. For an aspiring subject matter expert, writing and publishing on those topics is one of the best ways to develop domain expertise.

Littler's investment in building a substantial knowledge management (KM) department is one of its significant advantages and critical resources. Our KM department was established in 2001. Currently, Littler has over 20 dedicated knowledge management counsel (all attorneys with significant employment and labor experience). We also have dedicated research attorneys and over 25 professionals on our research and library team. All work together to generate a vast amount of legal content that is valuable to our attorneys and clients.

Within this larger group, we have a dedicated content publishing team that is responsible for producing initial drafts, reviewing content with attorney subject-matter experts, editing the content received from SMEs, and preparing and formatting content for publication. To ensure quality, most content generated by Littler attorneys is reviewed prior to publication by our publications review committee – a group consisting of knowledge management counsel and over 50 attorneys from across the firm, representing most of our major practice areas.

In addition to Littler's knowledge management department, the firm's marketing and business development (MBD) department plays an equally critical role in Littler's content marketing strategy. The MBD team oversees the distribution of Littler's content through its numerous online channels and manages the many content distribution relationships Littler maintains with third parties, whether they be subscribers or syndicators, and increasingly we are using data analytics to refine our content distribution strategies. The MBD team further leverages Littler's content through an increasingly robust social media and public relations strategy that takes full advantage of the brand-building opportunities social media provides.

Innovative legal service solutions as a brand differentiator for Littler

While a comprehensive content marketing program that provides clients and prospective clients with critical legal information plays an important role in a firm's innovation strategy, it is only one prong of a broader strategy. The firm must also demonstrate by its actions – as well as in its marketing – that it is committed to innovation, by being willing to change the way clients and lawyers work together.

About 15 years ago, Littler began taking its KM strategy to the next level. Using many of the same teams and enhanced content, we began building online tools – "service solutions" – that would give clients direct access to the firm's knowledge management and other useful resources. Our first major effort was Littler GPS®, an online subscription service that provided clients with access to a comprehensive database of multi-jurisdiction surveys – covering topics as diverse as minimum wage requirements or lactation accommodation obligations across every major US jurisdiction. Because employment law requirements are often state-specific, employers need to be aware of the various requirements across the jurisdictions in which they operate. Eventually, Littler GPS grew to cover over 90 employment law topics and included weekly updates of new legislative and regulatory developments in any jurisdiction.

Next, we began to provide online toolkits providing clients with access to information and resources covering specific industries and subject areas. For example, our Home Care Toolkit provides online compliance resources for employers in the home health care industry. Our Littler X-celerator™[7] provides start-up companies with access to resources to help them keep their growing businesses compliant with federal and California employment laws.

To aggregate our many content offerings into an integrated platform to serve our clients, we launched *Littler Edge*,[8] a comprehensive portal that enables clients to access Littler's many knowledge management services, including Littler GPS, the Littler On library, Littler's comprehensive collection of employee lifecycle documents (employment forms, policies, templates), links to required government employment forms, and other resources that enhance the ability of HR professionals and in-house employment counsel to meet their daily challenges. Littler Edge is provided on a complimentary basis to most Littler clients.

Over the past decade, Littler has gone beyond merely delivering content and legal information in innovative ways; the firm has become committed to delivering legal services to its clients in innovative ways leveraging technology, alternative staffing, and process reengineering. One of Littler's most transformative offerings is Littler CaseSmart®,[9] which, in our view, represents the future of employment law. It is a completely re-imagined process for managing administrative charges, single-plaintiff litigation, and employment law class actions. It combines proprietary technology – developed by Littler's industry-leading applications development team – an alternative staffing model, and a completely differentiated workflow process for handling legal matters. In the past decade we have handled over 30,000 administrative charges and litigation matters using this process, providing our clients with significant cost savings as well as transparent access to matter management and data analytics that enable them to analyze their matter portfolio and benchmark how they compare to other companies in their industry in terms of risk and litigation exposure.

Leveraging the proprietary technology platform developed for Littler CaseSmart, Littler's applications development team developed additional tools to enable clients to enhance legal compliance and their internal processes. Littler's Pay Equity Assessment™[10] measures compensation differences between demographic groups, identifies those that are statistically significant, and determines the extent to which these differences reflect legitimate business considerations. This provides clients with an analysis that assesses litigation risks and helps clients move toward achieving pay equity in their workforce. Littler's Restructuring Assessment Solution enables attorneys to methodically guide clients through the risks associated with workforce restructuring, automating adverse impact analyses, and producing insightful visual reports.

Littler OnDemand®[11] is a technology-based platform that provides answers to workplace questions and critical data analytics, leveraging Littler's OnDemand counsel – experienced employment law practitioners who average 15 years of legal experience and who are on call to answers common workplace questions.

ComplianceHR[12] is a unique joint venture between Littler and Neota Logic, a leading legal technology software provider. ComplianceHR's suite of products enable in-house counsel to efficiently handle routine requests from their internal HR and business unit clients, answering important but repetitive questions such as whether a given employee qualifies as overtime exempt or whether an individual can lawfully be engaged as an independent contractor. ComplianceHR offers a comprehensive tool, powered by Littler's subject matter experts, that enables employers to develop and keep up to date their employee handbooks and personnel policies. ComplianceHR also offers applications that generate routine documents such as employment agreements, NDAs, and non-competes. In 2020, responding to the COVID-19 pandemic, ComplianceHR launched CHR SmartScreen™,[13] which enables employers to send jurisdiction-specific health-symptom questionnaires to employees' smartphones each day before they come into the office and can track vaccination and testing status and requests for vaccination exemptions based on disability or religious beliefs.

In 2021, Littler's internal Innovation Advisory Council (IAC) launched Innovate 100, a hackathon-like tournament open to associates across Littler's US and global offices. The goal of the tournament was to emphasize that innovation is not the job of any one person or any one committee; those on the front lines of delivering legal services to clients know best where the current inefficiencies are and which solutions would best improve client service.

At the start of the tournament, associates were invited to form teams within their offices or practice groups and submit proposals for novel projects – involving technology solutions, business development ideas, opportunities to enhance client service delivery, or other innovations in our practice. From the 20 submissions received, the IAC selected four projects to advance in the competition. Over the next 100 days, the four teams worked to flesh out their ideas assisted by "mentors" including subject matter experts and members of the firm's corporate staff with relevant expertise depending on the nature of the project. Finally, the teams presented their completed projects to a panel of judges, both from within and outside of Littler, who awarded prizes for best presentation, best design, and best overall project. One of the projects was immediately approved for further development and several others will be developed and deployed.

Conclusion

These various initiatives represent Littler's efforts to provide unique and innovative services to its clients, recognizing that many legal services will inevitably move to an online service delivery model; not overnight, but over time. We are attempting to emulate and move with clients to the web-based service delivery model that is now the norm in virtually every other industry.

Of course, there will always be a need for trusted advisors – lawyers who can work with clients to develop bespoke strategies and solutions, delivering premium advice and counseling. While we know that there are limits to the services that can be delivered to clients online, we strongly believe that being at the forefront of developing unique legal services in ways that can help our clients be more successful demonstrates a genuine commitment to client service. It is also a reflection of our commitment to making innovation a key part of our brand.

References

1. Susskind, R., *Tomorrow's Lawyers: An Introduction to Your Future*, Oxford University Press, 2013.
2. www.littler.com/bookstore
3. www.littler.com/news-analysis
4. www.littler.com/publication-press/publication/annual-report-eeoc-developments-fiscal-year-2020
5. www.littler.com/publication-press/publication/wpi-labor-day-report-2021
6. www.littler.com/publication-press/publication/inaugural-report-littlers-global-workplace-transformation-initiative
7. www.littler.com/innovation/littler-x-celerator-toolkits
8. www.littler.com/innovation/littler-edge
9. www.littler.com/innovation/littler-casesmart
10. www.littler.com/innovation/littler-pay-equity-assessment
11. www.littler.com/innovation/littler-ondemand
12. https://compliancehr.com/
13. https://compliancehr.com/solutions/smartscreen/

Chapter 10: The LawNet Mark of Excellence – lessons for law firms

By Helen Hamilton-Shaw, member engagement and strategy director, LawNet

The worldwide COVID-19 pandemic has driven unprecedented transformation in every aspect of our day-to-day lives and in how we work with clients to deliver services. From the start of the first lockdown in March 2020, we saw firms in LawNet, our independent law firm network, embracing a major shift to digital activity, as they seized the initiative to find ways to connect with clients in the new, wholly online landscape. As clients showed they were open to innovation, firms accelerated the adoption of tech-based service solutions and we saw increasing take up in partnerships with leading edge providers by member firms keen to improve efficiency, communication, and client service. Amidst this fast-moving change, and mindful of the exceptional circumstances, our members did not lose sight of the importance of genuine relationships and an empathetic approach. This reflected the network's commitment to client satisfaction.

Strategically, it would be hard to disagree with international research and advisory firm Forrester,[1] which says prioritization of client experience to create and sustain loyalty will be more vital than ever in future. Forrester also points to the vital role research can play – both quantitative and qualitative – to understand behavior and guide future responses.

We see a customer-centric business model as one of the most important ways in which law firms can add value to what they already do, and it's why we created the LawNet Mark of Excellence,[2] which independently monitors and measures how firms engage with clients as part of our mandatory ISO quality standard. After eight years of independent monitoring, our firms have a huge bank of such data to draw on, as reported in "Lessons for law firms, the client experience".[3] This represents the sector's largest research project, with around 80,000 client satisfaction surveys completed and more than 6,500 customer experience (CX) reviews,[4] where independent researchers pose as potential clients. From the early days of walk-ins and telephone reviews, firms are now tested on everything from live chat to their appearances at business events. A further important development was the integration of the client survey benchmarking process with the ReviewSolicitors[5] online review site in 2016.

Online client reviews, survey feedback, CX researcher reports, and audio recordings combine to create a picture of the different stages of the client journey, helping firms to understand the client perspective and identify areas for improvement. Firms receive one-to-one feedback and in-house training to help them respond to the findings and develop sector-leading experiences, and our evidence shows this approach generates significant performance improvements.

At the heart of this is a commitment to listening to clients and learning from what we hear, skills that are paramount in the way ahead. We identified some years ago that such a culture, placing the client at the heart of a firm, could be a key differentiator for the mid-size independent law firm members in our collaborative non-profit network. Importantly for our firms, it's not about more compliance; it's about helping them meet the challenges of increased competition head-on, by enabling them to use their LawNet membership to make themselves stand out, without sacrificing their independence, individual identity, and brand.

The LawNet Mark of Excellence

At the outset of the project, we recognized that measurement was vital, as with any outcome-focused activity. No single metric can tell the whole story; rather, you need to consider the building blocks that comprise a positive experience – such as satisfaction, engagement, loyalty, and effort. By incorporating key measurement tools, we could help firms gather feedback and then help them focus on how they could use the metrics to drive real performance improvements. This was the underpinning of the development of our Excellence Mark, a charter mark that is now an integral part of our ISO 9001 standard, which means that customer service is audited across all LawNet firms.

Independently-conducted client research and experience reviews are key to our charter mark, to provide data that can be used to set our firms apart, unlike the many unsubstantiated claims made of "excellent" or "quality" service across the sector. Moreover, as we were looking to create a truly differentiating accreditation, we recognized that collecting and measuring customer satisfaction feedback was not an end in itself, and that learning and developmental support for change had to be an intrinsic part of the program.

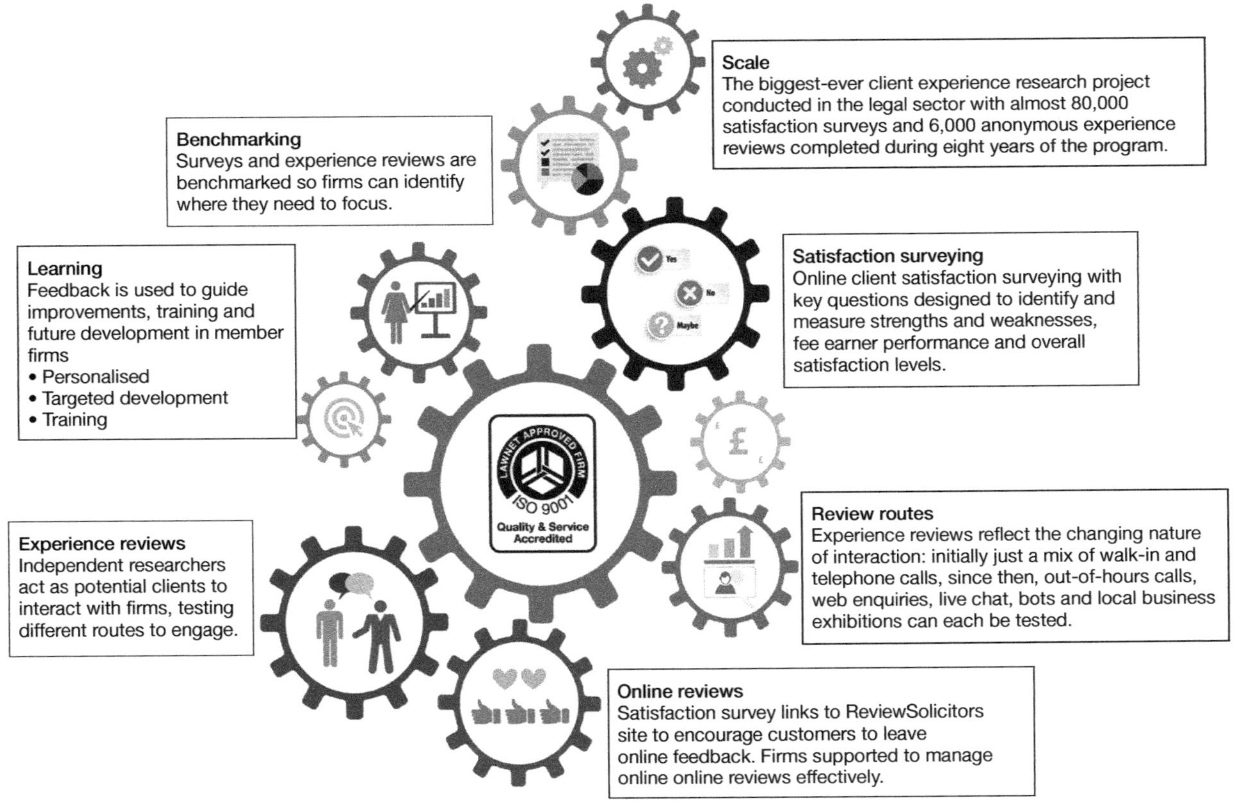

Figure 1: The inter-related components of the LawNet Mark of Excellence.

To get buy-in initially, we focused on regular communications and focus groups, which helped create a groundswell of member support prior to launch. To secure firm-wide awareness and adoption, we identified client service champions within each of the firms and gave them the support they needed internally. Apart from some inevitable minor teething problems, firms have been very receptive and positive about the Excellence Mark since its introduction, seeing the value of its long-term ambition.

Using dialogue with members to shape the development of the Excellence Mark reflected the approach we encourage in our firms, of listening to clients and shaping their offering to meet the needs identified.

A framework for developing your service proposition in this way is Design Thinking, which employs an empathetic, human-centric approach based on continual testing of ideas through dialogue with customers. By better understanding the unmet needs of customers, you are more likely to identify solutions that are revolutionary rather than incremental, while reducing the associated risks of trying new things. At a simple level it requires a shift from "this is what we do" to "how might we enable value to our users?"[6] and we see such co-creation as the way ahead.

Tracking and evaluating the journey made by clients can deliver a rich understanding and open the way to holistic customer-centric service delivery. Mapping should draw on client experience at each touchpoint, from the first contact onwards. By shifting the perspective away from a simple end-of-matter assessment to a wider, more strategic, focus, firms are more likely to identify gaps in processes or uncover where things break down.

Different clients have different journeys, so they need to be identified by demographics, such as age or geography, or by firmographics like industry sector. The journey will be different depending upon which service is being used or how they engage – whether online, by telephone, or face-to-face. Our member firms report that creating identifiable personas for different client types can be useful.

Similarly, how a firm interacts before, during, and after the engagement is vital and we have seen our member firms introduce a range of technology solutions to improve communication at each stage. In one firm, a multi-channel approach sees a variety of apps keep clients up to speed with case progress, along with an online live chat function.

For our members, regular client experience reviews are a requirement, with independent researchers acting as potential clients to interact with firms. The routes used by the researchers to make their enquiries include telephone, unscheduled walk-ins, web contact, live chat, and out-of-hours,

Creating a client journey map identifies every point of contact between your firm and your clients

This is just one example of a firm-wide overarching communications journey. Also, great insight can be achieved by mapping specific types of services.

As clients interact with a firm, they will have different experiences at different touchpoints along the journey. Touchpoints could be internally-managed points such as your website, chatbots, emails, phonecalls, events, client meetings and correspondence or externally-hosted online reviews, social media and advertisements.

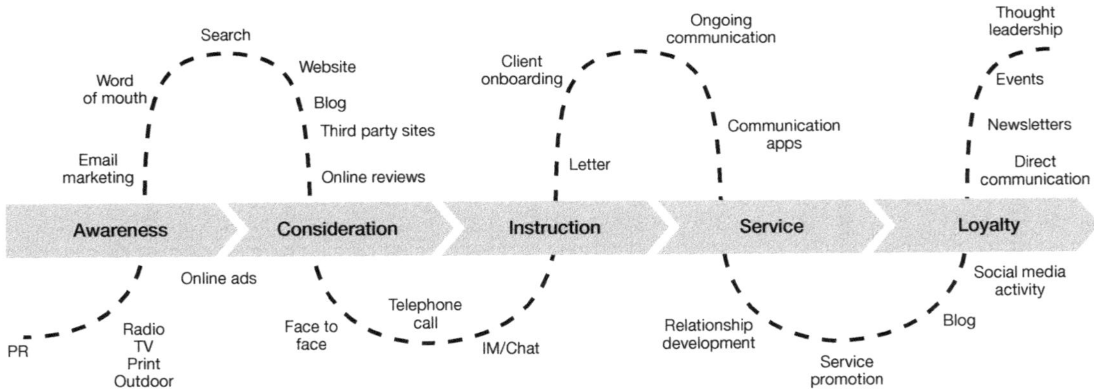

Top tips

1. Map out all the touchpoints of interaction with clients, from the first to the last.
2. Understand how clients navigate across touchpoints through the journey.
3. Identify the messages and experiences they receive at each touchpoint.
4. Think about needs, expectations, and desires and compare with actual experience at each stage.
5. Identify what is working and what is not.
6. Works out solutions to address gaps and opportunities that can improve the journey.

Figure 2: Map the client journey – one example of firm-wide communications touchpoints.

with samples taken across different departments throughout the year, equating to a monthly check-in, but avoiding any regular pattern that firms could identify and respond to. The reviews are delivered through the professional services division of insight6,[7] which provides one-to-one feedback and in-practice training to support findings.

Alongside, the client satisfaction surveying is conducted through LawLeague,[8] an independent portal, generating statistical data for firms to benchmark performance within their firm, across the network, and against other non-member firms. It also incorporates an integrated link to enable clients to self-publish an online review as they complete the survey.

The core purpose of our research is to help our firms identify where they can make improvements – and provide support to do so. Importantly, firms know that once changes have been made, they can measure impact in the next set of results that will benchmark their progress and attainments against their peers, both within the network and in the broader legal community.

Cultural commitment

Today's consumers of legal services are looking for great professional expertise and outstanding customer service, but equally important is confidence in a firm's purpose and personality. We know from our own research[9] that two-thirds of new business is generated through reputation and trust, which aligns with analysis in the broader economy, such as the Edelman Trust Barometer.[10] Similarly, international research and advisory firm Forrester[11] found that 57 percent of people were more likely to purchase and remain loyal to a brand that behaves well.

What our data has shown from the start is the importance of a firm-wide commitment to delivering excellent service, and that can only be achieved by truly understanding what clients want. In the first detailed analysis of our research, we found firms were receiving high scores for technical expertise and delivering positive outcomes, but by drilling down with clients below this headline performance, firms were able to identify and target those areas with the most potential to increase satisfaction, such as speed of response, upfront clarity on timescales and fees, combined with regular progress and cost reporting.

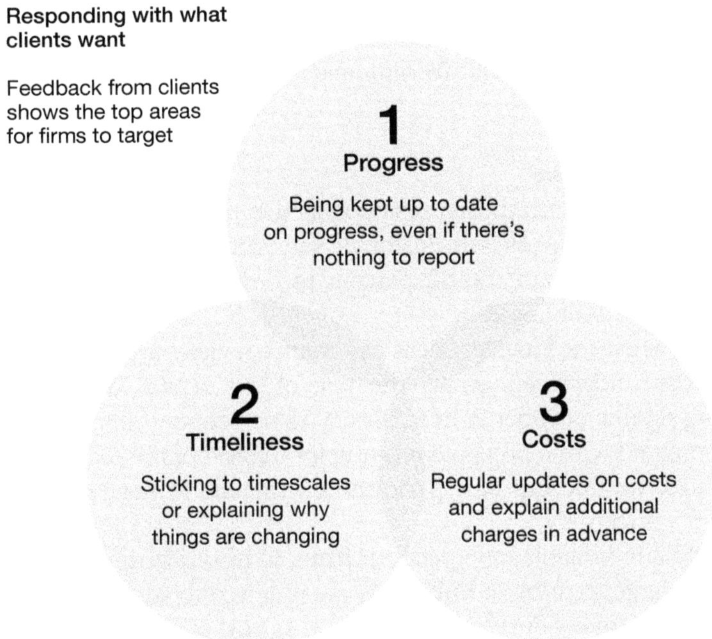

Figure 3: The priority areas that clients want firms to address at the outset.

The feedback also highlighted a need for greater emphasis on sales follow-up by firms. Qualitative feedback from client experience reviews showed that, where follow-up processes were not adhered to, clients interpreted it as a lack of interest, and firms were unlikely to convert the business. Having a great service proposition is all very well, but enquiries need to be captured and followed up, as there is little point investing resources in marketing and business development to generate leads for the firm if your enquiry management process lets them slip away.

Interestingly, the price quoted for a job is cited consistently as one of the least important factors in the decision to appoint a firm – a mere four percent of respondents quote cost as the main reason for instructing the firm[12] – with recommendation or previous contact being the most persuasive factors.

It is 20 years since loyalty guru Frederick Reichheld demonstrated how a five percent increase in customer retention could increase profits by more than 25 percent, because return customers tend to buy more from a company over time and will tend to refer others.[13]

This emphasis on reputation is reflected in the research undertaken by the Legal Services Consumer Panel (LSCP),[14] lending weight to the need for firms to provide consistency of service, of a high enough quality, if they are to secure those vital recommendations and repeat instructions consistently.

Rates of satisfaction

Comparing our data with the figures published in June 2021 by the LSCP,[15] our members show an overall customer satisfaction rate of 97 percent, substantially higher than the 83 percent recorded by the users of legal services canvassed for LSCP.

Similarly, when the LawNet client experience reviews are benchmarked against those undertaken across the rest of the sector, our firms are performing significantly better here, with a 68 percent overall performance rating, compared with a 58 percent rating for the rest of the sector. Within these figures, we find our best performing firms are achieving ratings in excess of 85 percent.[16]

It would be reasonable to expect our firms to record better results than the sector at large, bearing in mind they are required to adopt a structured approach to improving customer satisfaction as part of our mandatory ISO 9001 standard, but the statistics provide clear evidence that targeted measurement and support can drive significant performance improvements. This is evidenced by today's audited performance scores, compared with the start of the program, as illustrated in the statistics.

Overall, across the network, performance in the client experience reviews improved by 16 percent between 2012-13 and 2019-20, and the year-on-year detail shows a striking picture of how and where the program has driven improvement. For example, in the year after receiving their first audit results, firms achieved an impressive seven percent performance increase overall, by focusing on the areas identified as needing attention.

Drilling down into the 150+ individual criteria measured, many areas have shown exceptional improvements after being highlighted as important through the experience reviews and subsequent training. Having access to these detailed aspects of performance enables nuanced attention, such as the way that staff approach potential sales leads, by asking for permission to follow up on the enquiry, which recorded a massive 41 percent improvement in a single year. Much of the improvement is being driven by the program's focus on stronger sales skills, with firms demonstrating they know how to differentiate themselves, explain value, and justify price.

When firms are listening and learning from clients at every stage the most progress is made, and it was this holistic approach that saw the integration of the ReviewSolicitors site with our benchmarked customer

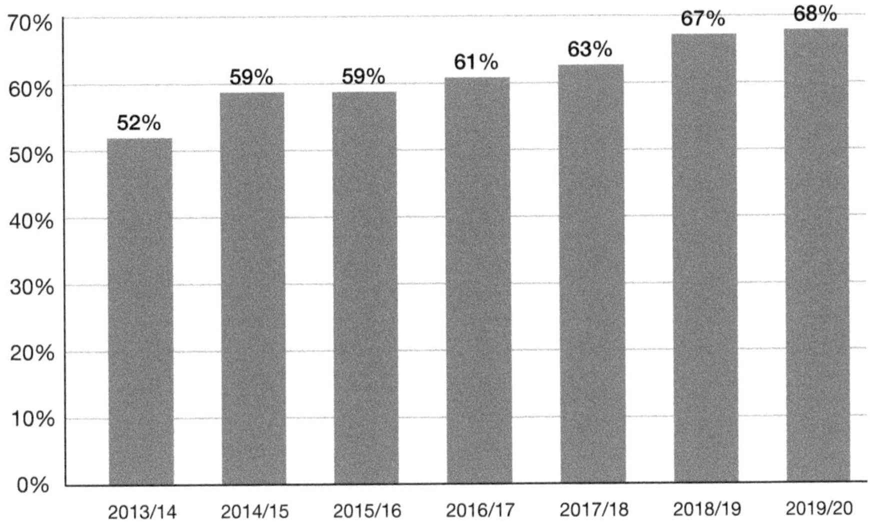

Figure 4: Overall client satisfaction rates: performance improvement in response to client experience review findings.

surveying process. This early adoption of online reviews, with clients actively encouraged to leave reviews and firms supported in developing techniques to make the most of positive feedback and manage any criticism effectively, has seen our network member firms dominate the rankings.

Learning lessons

Of course, not all reviews are positive. January 2021 saw the outcome of the defamation action[17] by law firm Summerfield Browne after a client left a negative review on Trustpilot saying, "A total waste of money another scam solicitor" [sic]. The firm was awarded £25,000 in damages and the court ordered that the defamatory review be removed.

The firm described a "measurable decline" in the number of enquiries in the weeks following the publication of the review, but Trustpilot said it had not been contacted by Summerfield Browne, nor had the review been flagged using its complaints process for reporting issues. This demonstrates why it is so important to be strategic and proactive in dealing with online commentary, rather than firefighting later.

While it can be tough hearing how you have performed in a review visit, or seeing what customers thought about your service, facing the facts can bring real value as we've seen from the changes implemented by members of the LawNet community.

Many of our firms find audio recordings of CX reviews between a

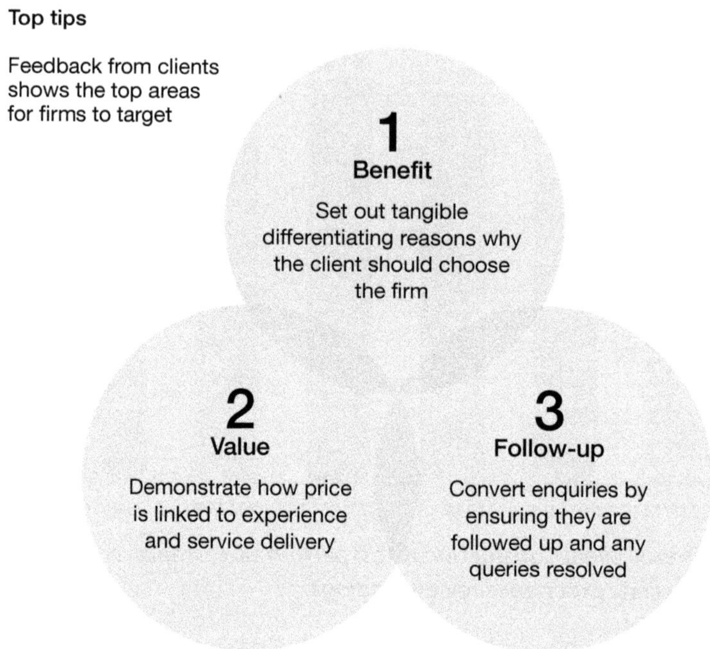

Figure 5: Clients identified key areas where firms could improve their ongoing communication.

researcher and fee earner hugely useful when placed in a culture that supports learning from the customer experience. Standing in the shoes of the potential client helps identify areas for individual skills development. We have seen members develop a bank of support resources or crib sheets to help prompt fee earners when engaging with clients, which can be a useful way of helping everyone deliver a consistently great experience. Equally, some may benefit from structured learning to tackle specific skills.

Lawyers often see negotiating as part of their core skillset, a fundamental part of their day-to-day business – mediating and negotiating between their client and the opposing side, whether a former spouse, employee, or supplier. However, when it comes to negotiating with a client on costs, there's often a big skills gap, according to our research.

Our client experience review measures this aspect, asking, "Did the team member confidently overcome the matter of cost?". The purpose is to identify any gaps in negotiation skills at a crucial stage in the sales process, to see whether the lawyers concerned were able to describe the value proposition for their firm and were comfortable in addressing a challenge on pricing without resorting to discounting. This is an issue that responds

Feedback from LawNet member firms on how they are making use of CX metrics to effect change:

Paint the vision
When putting measurement techniques in place, it's essential to paint a picture of what great service looks like for your clients, and how that translates for fee-earners and the firm.

Create the right culture
A firm-wide commitment to the process, with the pursuit of excellence and continual improvement embedded in the firm's culture, will have a big impact on effective outcomes.

Reward participation
It's uncomfortable to be scrutinized, and may cause a barrier to open communication, ongoing learning, and improvements. Demonstrating that you understand this, and that you're grateful, can help keep people on board.

Accentuate the positive; whilst improving the not-so-good
Any measurement program should highlight good performance, share best practice, and create opportunities to congratulate people on doing a great job, while also flagging up areas for improvement.

Share the results
It's vital that results are recognized as valuable learning for the whole firm and shared with everyone in an open and objective way, not restricted to individual managers or teams.

well to targeted action, with firms showing significant improvements once they recognize the need to develop skills.

Similarly, where our research showed customers wanted to be informed of the progress of jobs and resulting charges, one firm encouraged each team to take ownership, with benchmarks for service delivery. The result was much improved scores in customer feedback and more efficient working, with a reduction in time spent dealing with invoice queries, as the customer already knew what to expect.

These are granular examples, but several of our firms have won awards for their client care since the Excellence Mark was integrated into our ISO standard, by exhibiting a rounded, holistic approach that is driving results and setting them apart. Culture fuels change, and organizations that prioritize skills development and employee engagement in this way will be the ones to reap the rewards.

Your clients are your greatest advocates: understanding their motivations and experiences at every stage of their journey lies at the heart of a client-centric approach that will power your long-term strategic growth.

References

1. Forrester: European Predictions 2021 https://go.forrester.com/europe-predictions-2021-webinar
2. www.lawnet.co.uk/membership-benefits/practice-support/excellence-mark-client-care
3. www.lawnet.co.uk/media/2691/lawnet-client-experience-white-paper-2019.pdf
4. At May 2021.
5. www.reviewsolicitors.co.uk
6. Design thinking: www.designkit.org/methods/how-might-we
7. www.insight6.com/
8. www.law-league.com/
9. LawNet Excellence Mark research 2013-2020: www.lawnet.co.uk/membership-benefits/practice-support/client-experience-white-paper-2019
10. Edelman Trust Barometer: www.edelman.co.uk
11. Forrester Consulting, on behalf of Braze: www.braze.com/resources/library/report/what-makes-a-brand-human
12. LawNet Excellence Mark research 2013-2020: www.lawnet.co.uk/membership-benefits/practice-support/client-experience-white-paper-2019
13. Bain & Company, *The Loyalty Effect: The Hidden Force Behind Growth, Profits, and Lasting Value*, Harvard Business School Press, 1996 (Revised 2001): www.bain.com/Images/BB_Prescription_cutting_costs.pdf
14. www.legalservicesconsumerpanel.org.uk/what-we-do/research-and-reports
15. LSCP Consumer Tracker 2012-2021: www.legalservicesconsumerpanel.org.uk
16. LawNet Excellence Mark research 2013-2020: www.lawnet.co.uk/membership-benefits/practice-support/client-experience-white-paper-2019
17. *Summerfield Browne Ltd v. Waymouth* (2021) EWHC 85 (QB) (18 January 2021) www.bailii.org/ew/cases/EWHC/QB/2021/85.html

Chapter 11: Litigation management in a still uncertain world

By Paul A. Williams, partner and general liability litigation practice co-chair, Shook, Hardy & Bacon LLP

In 2020, the world began battling the COVID-19 pandemic. We endured lockdowns with stay-at-home orders that eventually gave way to cautious forays back into the world, taking baby steps to resume activity outside our homes. Our daily lives were guided by local health mandates prescribed by multi-colored COVID-19 risk levels providing an array of limitations, restrictions, and hopeful opportunities for our economic, professional, and social return, all of which ebbed and flowed with the surging waves of positive cases, outbreaks, and hotspots. Vaccines arrived, and it seemed an end must be near. But even now, a full return to "normal" remains elusive as the world battles the COVID-19 variants. We are caught in limbo between work-from-home and return-to-work, masks or no masks, and more restrictions loom large as the pandemic rages on and our children return to school. But life, business, and the legal practice presses on. Trials are coming back on calendar, the backlog is being worked, and pandemic-invoked litigation is already here with more still on the way. For many companies, litigation is inevitable, and with the pandemic, litigation is likely even less avoidable. But even so, the traditional burdens associated with litigation can be strategically managed to mitigate their impact on the company, its people and operations. With the right law firm partner you can achieve some certainty in a still uncertain world.

Pandemic litigation trends so far

As anticipated, the pandemic has prompted a surge of litigation,[1] which is a predictable result of illnesses, deaths, furloughs and layoffs, business shutdowns, and a general economic downturn. Perhaps more remarkable are the types of litigation that shape the leading edge of the surge, and those that trail behind and are yet to be filed.[2]

Litigation stemming from individuals contracting COVID-19 and alleging that a business is responsible because it failed to implement sufficient safeguards has largely focused on certain industries. Early in the pandemic, passengers filed over 100 individual and class action lawsuits against operators of cruise ships that experienced COVID-19 outbreaks. Nursing homes and others involved in senior care continue to face a steady stream of wrongful death claims, which make up more than half of all exposure claims. Some employers have faced take-home exposure claims that typically allege a person died of COVID-19 after contracting the illness from a spouse or family member who was exposed at work, though these remain rare. In some instances, employees or others have brought public nuisance claims, asserting that a business' operation poses an unreasonable risk of exposure.

Several factors have likely contributed to COVID-19 exposure claims not yet materializing at the level anticipated. First, state workers' compensation systems generally provide the exclusive remedy for workplace injuries aside from cases involving intentional misconduct. Second, plaintiffs face a challenge when attempting to prove causation. Third, whether voluntarily or as a result of government orders, limitations on large events reduced the potential for mass exposures. Finally, roughly two-thirds of states adopted some form of liability protection from COVID-19 exposure suits. These laws vary significantly from state to state, but generally provide a defense to businesses that follow public health guidance, raise the standard of liability beyond bare negligence, or combine these approaches.

While employees have brought relatively few personal injury claims against employers stemming from COVID-19, the same cannot be said of employment litigation, which makes up the largest share of all pandemic-related litigation. About one-third of COVID-19 employment litigation involves employees who claim employers improperly terminated them when they contracted COVID-19 or needed to quarantine, did not provide federally mandated paid sick leave, or failed to provide reasonable accommodations for employees with pre-existing medical conditions such as permitting them to work from home. The next most common employment suits allege that a business terminated an employee for expressing concerns about workplace safety or reporting an employee for not following public health guidance in violation of public policy. Changes in work schedules have led to a significant amount of wage and hour litigation. Some litigation contends that employers failed to pay employees for time spent taking COVID-19 tests or undergoing health screenings before work, for example. Given the number of layoffs, a significant portion of COVID-19 employment litigation involves employees who claim that their age, gender, race, or pregnancy was the true reason for their termination, some of which point to their employer later filling their position with someone in a non-protected class. Finally, some employment cases allege that an employer did not provide federally mandated paid family leave to those who were unable to work due to the need to care for a child whose school or daycare provider closed or was unavailable because of the pandemic.

Contract claims comprise about one-quarter of all COVID-19-related litigation, excluding employment and insurance litigation. Aside from general disputes stemming from the inability to fulfill contractual obligations during the pandemic, the most common contract litigation, in order of frequency, are claims seeking refunds for events such as weddings, other events or travel; disputes over commercial leases; and disputes over COVID-19-related products, such as a failure to supply masks that met specifications or deliver promised personal protective equipment at all.

There is also substantial insurance litigation. Most of this litigation involves whether a policyholder's business interruption insurance policy covers losses stemming from shutting down or scaling back operations during the pandemic. The issue in many of these cases is whether these losses stem from a physical loss or damage to the property, as many policies require. This litigation has slowed, with most courts finding in favor of insurers. Some lawsuits also target auto insurers, alleging that they should have refunded a portion of policyholder premiums due to the reduction in vehicle traffic during the pandemic.

There have been few COVID-19-related product liability claims, which could target the safety of vaccines or COVID-19 treatments, or the design or labeling of respirators, for example. The PREP Act, a federal law in place prior to the pandemic and implemented during COVID-19 through the US Department of Health and Human Services, provides robust liability protection to those who make, sell, distribute, or administer covered countermeasures.[3] In addition, several states have adopted product liability protections that extend to products, parties, or circumstances that may not be covered by the federal law. These laws discourage product liability lawsuits, though there have been government enforcement actions targeting price gouging and fraud, and consumer class actions targeting whether disinfecting or other products provide protection from COVID-19.

While the surge of COVID-19 hospitalizations, staffing and bed shortages, and the need to postpone non-emergency elective surgery and treatment led to the potential for medical malpractice claims, outside the nursing home context, plaintiffs' lawyers have filed relatively few lawsuits against healthcare providers. They may be discouraged from doing so in all but the most egregious cases by Executive Orders issued by governors and legislation that, in most states, provides for liability only in cases of gross negligence or reckless misconduct.

Other areas of focus are likely to trend in the coming months, and still others are anticipated, which have yet to be filed.

What still lies ahead?

As the economy continues to reopen and as businesses resume more fulsome operations, many companies and consumers are financially unable to complete contracted-for purchases. Many businesses are dealing with deconstructed supply chains, piecing together the means to resume production and deliver products to the marketplace. Plants and offices are trying to do business while managing ongoing COVID-19 health and safety protocols, also challenged by shortage of personnel and the increasing risks presented by unvaccinated personnel. Business deals that stalled may still be unable to close and will ultimately collapse. Companies still may be forced to restructure, or seek the safe harbor of protected bankruptcy proceedings. And for those hundreds of companies that answered the call for repurposing their operations to supply critical medical and health care equipment and supplies to help save lives? They are front and center for claims related to the virus. As we know, millions of people have gotten sick, and hundreds of thousands have lost their lives in the United States. And now, even at the risk of more employees leaving companies, or even exiting the work force, vaccine passports and vaccine mandates are squarely in view as the nation grasps inch by inch to close the gap to resume a pre-pandemic way of life.

As if this social and economic tragedy wasn't enough, in the midst of these turbulent circumstances prompted by the pandemic, we know opportunists are already engaged, filing lawsuits seeking to capitalize on the already-vulnerable business community.[4] Data hackers and cybersecurity threats are also rampant. As companies reopen their workplaces, the new health and safety measures create a risk of a new wave of privacy litigation, no matter how essential such measures are to enable the reopening of the economy and a hopeful return to normal. The list goes on (and on). Without question, more litigation is on the way.

The litigation burden

Even in the best of times, litigation can impose a substantial burden on companies, consuming time and resources that preferably would be spent pursuing new business opportunities and growth. The impact of these traditionally encountered burdens is exacerbated in times of crisis when companies need "all hands on deck" to focus on recovering, resuming operations and, in some cases, just financially surviving the crisis.

Now is not the time for serial training of multiple law firms hired to help with one-off cases. Now is not the time for many different points of contact reaching into the business looking for help answering questions and making requests for information. And now is not the time for companies to exhaust already stretched-thin resources trying to corral law firms and coordinate a consistent strategy and litigation effort. Moreover, never is it a time to overspend on litigation when a more coordinated, less burdensome and holistic option is available that provides companies with better litigation outcomes and a better overall litigation experience.

For law department teams and business executives, you will be pleased to know there is a way to protect your company, while rebuilding and growing your business, and you can do so in a way that provides a better overall litigation experience in an environment compatible with your company's culture and business objectives. With a client-focused law firm partner, companies can take a holistic – and strategic – approach to manage and control their litigation and mitigate the impact of litigation on the company, its people, and its operations.

The litigation management solution

Sophisticated litigation management begins with identifying risks and limiting exposure by establishing clear legal and business objectives to guide business strategy. Key to this effort is transparency, trust, collaboration, and accountability. An authentic business relationship between in-house counsel and their partner law firm thrives with their mutual dedication to questioning the status quo to find a better way and right-fit solutions for the issues at hand. Whether day-to-day work on the cases, urgent calls to address crises, or energetic and creative collaboration sessions with the team to brainstorm how best to address an anticipated concern, with the right partner the combined team can be in sync, on point and work seamlessly together. When goals and interests align, the mutual business clients are the collective priority focus for the team.

A representative case study illustrates this philosophy and these concepts in real life. Approximately five years ago, a global product manufacturing company was managing through some unexpected outcomes, escalating legal spend, disparate legal results across the country, and an increasing burden on the business and business team resources. The company linked up with a client-focused law firm partner who, based on data-driven legal analytics and a deep dive triage of past and existing litigated cases, offered a fresh-eyes perspective and a smorgasbord of opportunities to engage with its business teams to improve operations, mitigate risks, and better manage and defend its claims and litigation.

The transformation began with an intensive study of the company's leading businesses to identify risks in operations and opportunities for improvement with short, mid-range and long-term benefits. The next level effort continued by harmonizing differences and leveraging best practices across the various company businesses. An action plan was developed and priorities established to implement solutions and add value to the businesses. The combined legal team engaged the business teams in the design department, on the plant floor, and in the offices across the company with a "we're here to help" approach, strengthening the rapport and trust essential for effective legal-business client relations.

On the litigation front, the company centralized its litigation docket with its partner law firm, and together, the combined legal team triaged the litigation portfolio, targeted priority objectives to relieve specific burdens on the company, and crafted a unified strategy for handling litigation related to both upstream and downstream products. The team also identified metrics that provided objective analytics to help visualize the success achieved and the value of proactive litigation management to its key stakeholders and investors.

Now, with a sophisticated litigation management approach fully integrated within the company's culture, the legal and business teams work more effectively together, with frequent outreach to support decision-making, before mistakes are made, and routine reporting on near misses and lessons learned to further mitigate future claims and litigation. The traditional litigation burden is reduced, and a continuous improvement program rewards creative innovation designed to further lighten the load as the teams move forward together with like-minds. Additionally, the company continues to experience a decrease in litigation cycle time and all-in spend with better and more consistent legal outcomes.

A sophisticated litigation management approach applies to all kinds of matters, including pandemic-driven matters. The model is not limited to mass tort or repetitive types of litigation. Rather, this model allows companies to strategically and holistically manage and control a diverse litigation portfolio. With a client-first law firm partner philosophically aligned with the company's legal and business objectives, that company can better control more than it thought possible, even in today's uncertain world.

The practice of successful litigation management

The key hallmarks of this model are described below. Leveraged by an experienced partner law firm with both the know-how and a client-first focus, these tools and tactics can deliver consistency, continuity, and predictability for a company's litigation docket. These practice principles are also rooted in transparency, trust, collaboration, and accountability, with innovation and incentive as the catalyst for a dynamic and engaging client experience.

Learn the company's business, issues and obstacles to design right-fit solutions

By knowing the industry and the business operations, outside counsel can anticipate, prepare, and effectively plan to mitigate risks and execute on exit strategies fit for the business.

Complete a strategic early case assessment to guide exit strategies consistent with the overall legal and business objectives

By front-loading the investigation and analyses, the legal and business teams can be better apprised of the risk and make more informed decisions about each case and about the portfolio of cases as a whole.

Use right-sized, right-fit, core team members, knowledgeable of the business, goals, issues and tactics

Teams comprising a balanced blend of industry background, institutional knowledge, and legal experience help ensure efficient, effective, and timely support for the litigation portfolio. Project management guidance and support, coupled with legal tools (and technology), are also crucial for an effective team.

Proactively manage the litigation

Being strategic and proactive by doing the right things at the right times the right way keeps the team actively progressing toward the exit strategies. Actively managing team members to ensure the necessary work activity stays true to the game plan and is performed at the right level is also critical to ensure optimal efficiency and predictable legal spend.

Leverage technology for effective legal project management

The past adage "don't reinvent the wheel" is no longer enough. Knowledge management is a given. Now outside counsel must actively direct workflow processes, employ artificial intelligence tools, utilize remote, sharable document and matter management platforms, and seamlessly dovetail file management with presentation tools for effective matter management and trial presentations.

Provide real time communication

Nothing is more team-building than constant, effective communication and collaboration with the combined legal team. Critical for team spirit and continuity, always celebrate successes and give credit where credit is due. It's a team effort, and everyone appreciates being appreciated. Also, integrating matter management systems and online file-sharing tools can facilitate routine reporting and information sharing with the combined legal team.

Vigorously seek improvement, innovating and adapting to achieve better results

Only by challenging the status quo and demanding exploration for better options, more effective ways of doing what needs to be done, can teams continue to reach the next level of achievement. Companies seek the same from their business teams, and expect ongoing valuable additions to the relationship.

Align pricing arrangements to keep the company and partner firm moving forward together

Pairing an aligned strategy with a pricing arrangement that incentivizes both the company and partner law firm to stay in sync sets the foundation for a win-win for both parties in the relationship. The arrangement(s) may have many facets, and may differ by practice area and project, but in sum, if the parties are motivated and financially incentivized in the same direction, the partnership is more assured of having a mutually successful outcome.

Provide lessons learned with practical solutions to mitigate future risk

A client-first partner helps avoid risks and exposures, literally reducing the need for the partner's legal services. That's what a client-first-focused partner does. Sharing information learned in litigation with the business teams helps the team members increase their awareness and improve their ability to self-identify and avoid repeat issues in the future. Additionally, if you see it, report it. For example, cure a gap in a form contract or recommend a necessary modification for a product label to mitigate future risk. Also, the active, real-time dialogue between the combined legal team and the business teams enhances the rapport between participants and leads to better, more effective communications and solutions and, most importantly, reduced risk from future litigation.

Quantify and capture metrics to objectively demonstrate the value provided to stakeholders Transparency, trust, collaboration, and accountability are critical elements of a sophisticated litigation management approach. These elements can and must be quantified, measured, and reported. The model works. The metrics will prove it. The stakeholders and investors will appreciate the value of continuity, consistency, and predictability in litigation. They will appreciate the better financial outcomes, too.

Finally, most law firms will do anything to avoid trial. But a client-focused law firm partner, equipped with the right experience, tools, tactics, and a sophisticated litigation management approach, will achieve your best available outcomes based on a credible threat of trial and trying cases that should be tried. Your legal and business objectives shape the exit strategy, and sometimes that means resolution before trial. But, when achieving your objectives requires a trial, you need a law firm capable of delivering results when it matters most. Under this model, each case is prepared in a manner that allows the company to decide its course, on its terms, and in its time, including trial. Trying the right cases – cases that should be tried – is a powerful tool that will help a company achieve its goals.

An opportunity to take control

Litigation is often inevitable, and with the pandemic, likely now even less avoidable, but the traditionally encountered burdens associated with it can be strategically managed to mitigate their impact on the company, its people, and operations. With a sophisticated litigation management approach and a client-first focused law firm partner, the business leaders can concentrate on the business and trust its combined legal team to holistically – and strategically – manage the company's litigation outcomes in a manner consistent with the company's culture and legal and business objectives. This model can provide a bit of certainty in a still uncertain world.

References

1. A special thank you to my law partner and friend, Cary Silverman, who has served at the tip of the spear in monitoring COVID-19 litigation across the United States and who has worked tirelessly to help develop, draft, support, and promote enactment of legislation to aid and protect businesses from liability exposure created by the COVID-19 pandemic.

2. The data presented in this chapter reflects our analysis of over 10,000 COVID-19 related complaints.
3. 42 U.S.C. 247d-6d; see also US Department of Health and Human Services, Public Readiness and Emergency Preparedness Act, www.phe.gov/Preparedness/legal/prepact/Pages/default.aspx (providing PREP Act Declaration of 17 March 2020, amendments to the Declaration, and advisory opinions that define the scope of liability protection).
4. My colleague and law partner, the renowned Victor Schwartz, spoke to concerns raised by these types of suits: www.washingtonexaminer.com/opinion/op-eds/trial-lawyer-greed-in-time-of-need.

Lightning Source UK Ltd.
Milton Keynes UK
UKHW020233220222
399045UK00006B/134

9 781787 428133